TWO ESSAYS ON STEPANOV DANCE NOTATION

BY

Alexander Gorsky

I. Table of Signs for the Notation of the Movements of the Human Body According to the System of the Artist of the Imperial St. Petersburg Theaters V. I. Stepanov.

II. Choreography: Examples for Reading.

Translated from the Russian by

Roland John Wiley

Noverre Press

First published in 1978 by CORD (Congress on Research in Dance)
and here reprinted with their kind permission by:

The Noverre Press
(A division of Dance Books Ltd.)
Southwold House
Isington Road
Binsted
Hampshire
GU34 4PH

© 2019 Roland John Wiley

ISBN 978-1-906830-87-8

FOREWORD

With these translations of Alexander Gorsky's essays on Stepanov Dance Notation CORD marks the beginning of its second decade of existence. This is the first study to appear under CORD's new name, the Congress on Research in Dance, Inc., and, moreover, inaugurates a new series of monographs to be called "CORD Special Publications." Forthcoming titles in this series will be issued on an open schedule, depending on the readiness of substantial works of new research and new editions of historical value.

Roland John Wiley, who translated Gorsky's essays and supplied the introduction and bibliography, received his Ph.D. in music from Harvard University. In addition to teaching at the University of Michigan, Ann Arbor, he has lectured on various aspects of Russian ballet and is currently preparing a book on the ballets of Tchaikovsky.

The Editorial Board of CORD
December 1977

The publication of these translations was supported

by

The Horace H. Rackham Endowment

of

The University of Michigan at Ann Arbor

and

The Capezio Foundation.

The translations were prepared from originals

in

The Harvard Theatre Collection.

CONTENTS

	Page
Foreword	iii
Translator's Preface	ix
Table of Signs for the Notation of the Movements of the Human Body According to the System of the Artist of the Imperial St. Petersburg Theaters V. I. Stepanov	[1]
Supplement to the Tables	[21]
Choreography; Examples for Reading	[25]
Notes to the Main Text	[71]
An Annotated Bibliography	[74]
Information About CORD	[77]

TRANSLATOR'S PREFACE

I. Stepanov, Gorsky, Sergeyev.

These treatises by Alexander Gorsky (1871-1924) represent an important stage in the development of movement notation in late imperial Russia, a bridge between the invention of a notation system and the actual recording of ballets. The sequence of invention, refinement and practical application in this case spanned the quarter century between 1891 and 1916, and resulted in the notation of a substantial portion of the Maryinsky Theater ballet repertoire from this period.[1] If knowledge of Gorsky's work will open the study of these extraordinary choreographic records to English-reading authorities, no further justification for the translations is needed.[2] But to understand them fully it is necessary to know the contributions of two other men, Vladimir Stepanov and Nikolai Sergeyev, and Gorsky's relationship to them.[3]

Vladimir Ivanovich Stepanov, who devised the notation system Gorsky describes, was born in St. Petersburg on 17 June 1866. For the next nineteen years of his life, until his graduation from the theater school, we know practically nothing about him. He entered the corps de ballet of the Maryinsky Theater on 3 May 1885, and by 1889 had advanced to first coryphée.[4]

His promise as a dancer must be guessed from brief statistics taken early in his career, for Stepanov soon developed another interest. In 1889 he petitioned the supervisor of the ballet company for permission to attend classes at the University of St. Petersburg, and for the next two years studied anatomy and anthropology there.[5] By 1891 he had

---

[1] Most of the notations are now preserved in the Harvard Theatre Collection, bMS (1) to (269), and fMS 186 (1) to (14). Besides choreographic notations (which vary in the degree of completeness), this group of documents, the so-called Sergeyev Collection, contains music, scenarios, programs, and other materials relating to the ballets.

[2] Strict transliteration has been retained hereinafter in footnote citations and the bibliography; in the main body of the text it has been relaxed in favor of spellings more typical of English usage: "Sergeyev" rather than "Sergeev," "Gorsky" and not "Gorskii," "Alexander" and not "Aleksandr," etc.

[3] This essay is based on available documentary sources. At such time as the archives of the imperial theaters and the Ministry of the Imperial Court, now preserved at the Central State Historical Archive in Leningrad, are more readily accessible, our knowledge of these men will doubtless be enriched.

[4] *Yearbook of the Imperial Theaters* [Ezhegodnik Imperatorskikh Teatrov], VI (Season 1895-1896), p. 505.

[5] Stepanov's petition is briefly quoted in Vera Mikhailovna Krasovskaya, *Russian Ballet Theater of the Second Half of the Nineteenth Century* [Russkii baletnyi teatr vtoroi poloviny XIX veka] (Moscow and Leningrad, 1963) [hereinafter: *KrasXIX*], p. 446. An account of Stepanov's life published at the time Gorsky produced *Sleeping Beauty* in Moscow from notations (see p. xiv), states that Stepanov began to produce a system of movement notation while still a student. See the *Moscow Gazette* [Moskovskie vedomosti], 26 January 1899, p. 4, cols. 5-6. Although the report is unsigned and no source is given for its information, the details that it alone provides, together with the possibility that it came directly from an interview with Gorsky (Stepanov's close friend), justify its

formulated a system of movement notation which he demonstrated successfully before officials of the ballet company (see below, p. xii). On the basis of this demonstration the theater directorate granted Stepanov a leave of absence and a modest stipend with which he traveled to Paris in May of 1891, to perfect his system by further study of anatomy.[6]

In Paris Stepanov worked with the important neurologist Jean Martin Charcot, who is said to have been impressed with the notation system, as was Joseph Hansen, balletmaster of the Opera who had once worked for the imperial theaters. Hansen endorsed Stepanov's invention in a letter that the young Russian reproduced in a supplement to the brightest achievement of his Paris trip—his book: *Alphabet des mouvements du corps humain. Essai d'enregistrement des mouvements du corps humain au moyen des signes musicaux.* But Stepanov paid for these accomplishments with borrowed money and his health.[7] Malnutrition is thought to have led to tuberculosis, which unquestionably contributed to his early death. He returned to St. Petersburg on 14 July 1892, and, possibly because he was convalescing, we know little of his activity for the remainder of the year. That he danced in only five performances of the 1892-1893 season may also relate to illness.

1893 brought Stepanov satisfactions both professional and personal. In April he successfully defended his notation system in a second, more elaborate trial examination (below, p. xiii), as a result of which it was made a course of study in the theater school and he the instructor.[8] Sometime during the year he married Maria Alexandrovna Erler, who graduated from the ballet school in the spring, and on 1 October he was promoted to second dancer. It seems, however, that Stepanov discontinued public performance entirely after the 1892-1893 season. It is likely too that Gorsky's friendship with Stepanov ripened at about this time.[9]

The next sign of official approbation for Stepanov's work came in the fall of 1895, when on 20 September he was dispatched to Moscow to introduce his system at the Bolshoi Theater School. While there he fell seriously ill and died on the night of 15-16 January 1896. His funeral followed on the 19th, at the Vagankov Cemetery.

---

citation here and in the next footnote. In the introduction to the *Table of Signs* Gorsky refers to Stepanov's meditations on the problem of movement notation while still a student.

Stepanov is also remembered for devising a program of graded classroom exercises for ballet training. It has been published in M. Borisoglebskii, ed., *The Past of the Ballet Division of the Petersburg Theater School, now the Leningrad State Choreographic School. Materials for the History of Russian Ballet* [Proshloe baletnogo otdeleniya peterburgskogo teatral'nogo uchilishcha, nyne Leningradskogo Gosudarstvennogo Khoregraficheskogo Uchilishcha. Materialy po istorii russkogo baleta], 2 vols. (Leningrad, 1938-1939) [hereinafter: *Borisoglebskii*], II, 260-262.

[6] Sources differ in recording the amount of Stepanov's stipend. Krasovskaya cites a state document that indicates 600 rubles (*KrasXIX*, p. 446); the *Moscow Gazette* article (cited in the previous note) emphatically states "400 rubles, no more." In either case it was very little.

[7] Dancer Aleksandr Aleksandrovich Oblakov (1862-1906) took an advance of 300 rubles on his own salary and sent it to Stepanov in Paris, and after his friend's death paid an 800-ruble debt Stepanov had left (*Borisoglebskii*, I, 303). Oblakov was also a member of the commission that recertified the notation system in 1893.

[8] 1 September 1893 is the date of Stepanov's official appointment as instructor in the school; Borisoglebsky claims, however, that he had been teaching his system informally for a year before the appointment was made (*Borisoglebskii*, II, 37, n. ****), a claim further substantiated in a newspaper report. *The New Time* [Novoe vremya] for 23 April 1893 (p. 3, col. 5) states, in part: "The artist of the ballet troupe Mr. Stepanov, having invented a system for notating body movements, *was at the beginning of the current school year* [*i.e.,* in August of 1892], invited to become a teacher of this system." Italics added.

[9] When Gorsky developed an interest in notation cannot be established, although one of his biographers suggests that it may have been in 1895. See Yurii Alekseevich Bakhrushin, *Aleksandr Alekseevich Gorskii, 1871-1924* (Moscow and Leningrad, 1946), p. 10. As members of the same company, Gorsky and Stepanov could have been acquainted with each other for several years before this.

Gorsky assumed Stepanov's teaching duties in St. Petersburg. While remembered also as a dancer and choreographer,[10] Gorsky has been described as "a fervent adherent of the new theory of choreography," who "took upon himself the moral responsibility to finish the work Stepanov had begun."[11] He progressed toward this goal by reworking the notation system to make its practical application to ballet more feasible, and by giving two more public demonstrations.

Gorsky continued to teach notation and to encourage its use until his transfer to Moscow in 1901. During his term as instructor some choreographies of the Maryinsky repertoire were recorded, but the absence of published documents about the matter prevents us from knowing when this labor began, whether it was systematic, or who authorized the expenditure of time and money for it.[12] Additional proof of the importance of the project may be inferred from the fact that in 1897, Gorsky was provided with an assistant, Nikolai Sergeyev.[13]

If Stepanov deserves credit for inventing the system and Gorsky for refining it, then Nikolai Grigorevich Sergeyev (1876-1951), despite self-serving motives attributed to him, must be acknowledged as the person who put it to best use. Like Gorsky, Sergeyev began as an apprentice and advanced to a teaching post on the departure of his master.[14] It was during Sergeyev's term as notation instructor (he was appointed regisseur in 1903 but continued in both positions concurrently) that the bulk of the surviving collection of notations was prepared.[15]

Sergeyev's personal behavior as an official of the imperial ballet during the last fifteen years of its existence has been too harshly criticized to be disregarded, although

---

[10] On Gorsky as dancer and choreographer (whom Soviet historians rank as equal in importance to Fokine), see, *e.g.*, Vera Mikhailovna Krasovskaya, *Russian Ballet Theater of the Beginning of the Twentieth Century* [Russkii baletnyi teatr nachala XX veka], 2 vols. (Leningrad, 1971-1972) [hereinafter: *KrasXX*], I, 107-151, 230-306; Natalia Petrovna Roslavleva, *Era of the Russian Ballet* (New York, 1966), pp. 155-166.

[11] Bakhrushin, *Aleksandr Alekseevich Gorskii*, p. 10. When Gorsky began teaching notation the title of the post was changed: Stepanov had been Instructor of "Theory and Notation of Dances," while Gorsky was simply Instructor of "Theory of Dances." The new title may have corresponded to some change in the substance of the course, for later in the cited passage Bakhrushin writes: "From 1897 Stepanov's system was introduced into the teaching plan of the school under the title "Theory of Dances," and Gorsky was designated instructor of this *new subject*" (italics added). Bakhrushin acknowledges in the immediately preceding sentences that Gorsky's appointment as a pedagogue coincided with the date of Stepanov's death.

[12] A survey of the surviving Stepanov notations reveals that work began on notating some ballets before Gorsky's transfer; some (such as the Petipa-Drigo *Talisman*) appear to have been started while Stepanov was still alive.

[13] As Borisoglebsky puts it: "In 1897 he [Sergeyev] was put in with the coryphées with annual pay of 700 rubles. In the very same year, in order to escape military service, Sergeyev obtained for himself, after much trouble, the place of assistant to the instructor of Stepanov dance notation in the theater school. Sergeyev agreed to be pedagogue without pay, in order not to go into military service" (*Borisoglebskii*, II, 76).

[14] Sergeyev seems to have taken over the teaching of dance notation before Gorsky's official transfer. In the *Yearbook of the Imperial Theaters* [Ezhegodnik Imperatorskikh Teatrov], [XI] (Season 1900-1901), p. 136 of the Register of Artists, we find (1) that Gorsky "left the service" (*i.e.*, was transferred to Moscow) on 1 January 1901, and (2) that Sergeyev was teacher of the "Theory of Notating Dances" [note that the title has changed again–*cf.* note 11 above] on 1 September 1900. Gorsky's transfer date may be an administrative technicality, for he was busy in Moscow producing ballets during much of the year 1900. See *KrasXX*, I, 115-117.

[15] Sergeyev's career and papers (the collection referred to above in note 1) are described by the present writer in "Dances From Russia: An Introduction to the Sergejev Collection," *Harvard Library Bulletin*, XXIV (1976), 94-112.

few substantiated proofs of wrongdoing have been published;[16] even his technical competence has been called into question.[17] Nevertheless, he was responsible for two critical developments in the practical application of the Stepanov system: the notation of a large number of ballets, and the introduction of these ballets, from notations, into repertoires of new companies.[18]

II. The Stepanov system in practice.

In the decades since its use in the imperial theaters was discontinued, Stepanov notation has come to be considered a historical curiosity.[19] Whatever the merits of this view, it is helpful to an understanding of Gorsky's treatises to realize how rigorously the system was examined, Gorsky's part in this examination, and to make at least a passing scrutiny of the reasons offered for its abandonment.

The first official recognition of the system is the protocol dated 24 February 1891, which, like Joseph Hansen's letter of endorsement, Stepanov reproduced in a supplement to his book. Its signatories, which included Marius Petipa, Lev Ivanov and other important figures in the imperial ballet, declare the system "useful and readily suitable for the notation of ballets." But neither this document nor any other published account specifies a practical test on which such an assessment was based. One newspaper referred to a "series of lectures in the classes of the theater school, in the presence of the artists and the entire staff of the commission,"[20] but no source indicates the preparation of an actual dance.

There are reasons to believe that the protocol was a formality. If the system had been fully practicable there would have been no reason to send Stepanov to Paris. If there had been no doubt of its usefulness Stepanov would not have been required to submit it to a more elaborate examinaton before school officials introduced it into the curriculum, and Gorsky, after Stepanov's death, would have had no need to offer public demonstrations of its utility twice again. Implicit is some official skepticism about the system, and we find evidence of this coming from Petipa himself. In a document dated 10 February 1892 he wrote:

> "I am a great admirer of all fine things, but not at all of skeletons, which have no place in the choreographic art. It is possible to find balletmasters who have the patience to revive previously produced dances with

---

[16] See, e.g., *KrasXIX*, p. 448; Roslavleva, *Era*, pp. 170-173, 197-198; *Borisoglebskii*, II, 76-79; Vladimir Arkad'evich Telyakovskii [the last Director of the Imperial Theaters], *Reminiscences* [Vospominaniya] (Leningrad and Moscow, 1965), pp. 241-242.

[17] See, e.g., Fedor Vasil'evich Lopukhov, *Candid Remarks About Choreography* [Khoreograficheskie otkrovennosti] (Moscow, 1972), p. 54; Ninette de Valois, *Come Dance With Me; A Memoir, 1898-1956* (London, 1957), pp. 110-112; Margot Fonteyn, *Autobiography* (New York, 1976), p. 70.

[18] Sergeyev began to produce revivals based on notations while still in the imperial theaters; in the west after the October revolution, he worked for the Diaghilev Ballets Russes, the Latvian National Theater in Riga, the Paris Opera and other companies, but most importantly for the Vic-Wells and the International Ballets. The extent to which Sergeyev himself notated ballets cannot be established—he was assigned two assistants for this purpose, and it is possible that his own role was principally that of supervisor.

[19] Leonide Massine uses the Stepanov system to notate examples in his *Massine on Choreography; Theory and Exercises in Composition* (London, 1976), but his purpose is not to describe Stepanov's method, which he modifies. See reviews of Massine's book by Ann Hutchinson Guest in *The Dancing Times*, LXII (1977) [the issue for April], 391, and Jillian Officer in *York Dance Review*, No. 6 (Spring 1977), pp. 49-51.

[20] *The New Time* [Novoe vremya], 10 March 1891, p. 4, col. 3.

the help of the method of Mssrs. Thoinot Arbeau, Feuillet, Pecours, St.-Léon, Zorn, Stepanov and others..., but I consider it extremely difficult to show, in one and the same measure, the position of the arms, head, pelvis, upper part of the hips, movements of the knees, torso, turns of the body, flexion and extension of the shoulders, hands, wrists, and so forth.

The talented balletmaster, reviving earlier ballets, will compose dances in conformity with his own fancy, his talent and the tastes of the public of his own time, and will not come to lose his time and effort copying what was done by others long before. We note that in *La Fille mal gardée* Mr. Taglioni changed all the previous dances, and Mr. Hertel composed new music, and so too do I, without exception, every time I revive an old ballet. And then, each dancer of course performs these dances depending on her manner and capabilities.... I am completely convinced (pray God that I may be wrong) that worthy balletmasters will not use the method of notation which Mr. Stepanov, by the way, did not discover."[21] [In his last remark Petipa is referring to his contention that Stepanov's system is really only an extension of Arbeau's, in that both depend on musical notation.]

One cannot contest Petipa's principal criticisms: that dancing is too complex to be recorded completely in any condensed system, and that notation runs counter to the tradition of composing for the gifts of a particular dancer. It is curious, however, that he should have signed the flattering protocol and then within a year have experienced such a change of mind. His disdain must be a factor in assessing the vitality of Stepanov notation, for opposition from the chief balletmaster cannot be dismissed lightly. (One wonders if Petipa might not have been piqued at rival Joseph Hansen's endorsement of the system in Stepanov's book.) Petipa was not among the authorities who re-examined the system in 1893, and there is nothing in later documents that bears witness to his approval of it.

Although the system's repeated trials and Petipa's diatribe against it suggest that theater officials doubted its value, some consideration must be given to evidence hinting at approval. Indeed, all of the actions taken by the directorate on Stepanov's behalf—from granting permission to audit courses to forming a commission to examine the system to introducing it into the school curriculum—must be taken as positive ones. The theater administration was under no obligation to encourage him at all, for Stepanov had no links to influential circles by birth, and its own bureaucracy was so inefficient that without special favor his invention could have been lost in administrative inertia at any time. That it survived at all is an indication of approval.

The next examination, in April of 1893, corrected the apparent deficiency of the first: it required a practical demonstration. This came in two installments eight days apart. In the first, so-called "theoretical" portion given on the 14th, students executed steps from notations that were prepared in their absence. In the second, "practical" portion Stepanov revived from notations Jules Perrot's *Délire d'un peintre* for an examination performance at the Maryinsky Theater.[22] "The result proved most brilliant," according to the reviewer of the *Petersburg Gazette*, "students would easily notate a

---

[21] Quoted from *Marius Petipa; Materials, Reminiscences, Articles* [Marius Petipa; materialy, vospominaniya, stat'i], ed. Yurii Iosifovich Slonimskii *et al.* (Leningrad, 1971), pp. 121-122. The editors give no information concerning the circumstances of Petipa's writing of this document, or what kind of document it is.

[22] This is one of several ballets known to have been notated (Gorsky's *Clorinda*, discussed below, p. xv, is another), but which do not survive in Sergeyev's papers now at Harvard. Stepanov's notations stemmed from Christian Johannson's recollection of the work (*KrasXIX*, p. 448).

dance theme assigned to them in the Stepanov system, and then other students so designated examined and danced the assigned theme.... An attempt was made to notate character dances also, and this too proved successful."[23]

It was, apparently, on the strength of this demonstration that theater administrators introduced Stepanov notation into the curriculum. This accomplished, official concern seems to have given way to other matters; we read nothing more of the system for the next few years. Then, in 1898, Gorsky was dispatched to Moscow to produce *Sleeping Beauty* for the Bolshoi Ballet. Some accounts permit us to believe that he did this from notations, and with Petipa's blessing.

The dates of Gorsky's work reveal it to be an astonishing feat. According to Bakhrushin, he was in Moscow from 3 to 17 December, and returned on 12 January 1899, with the first performance following five days later on the 17th.[24] On 15 December he addressed the company:

> "Today for the first time we are rehearsing the entire ballet *Sleeping Beauty*, and today I am seeing here together all of the participants in it. I hasten to convey to you a deep *révérence* and sincere greeting from the author of this ballet, the famous artist Marius Ivanovich Petipa, and I am taking the liberty, on his behalf, to thank you for that zeal, for that enthusiasm with which you, with my help, strove to recreate this choreographic work. I think that here it is more than timely to remember that modest hard-worker, our colleague, the deceased artist Vladimir Ivanovich Stepanov, who devoted his entire short life to the art dear to him. Thanks to his invention it was possible for me to notate this artistic work and in 9 days (a period less than short), in 17 rehearsals transmit it to you."[25]

A strict reading of Gorsky's address confirms neither that he actually produced *Sleeping Beauty* from notations, nor that Petipa in fact gave any forthright support to the proposal of reconstructing the work in this way. Because Gorsky prepared his remarks as well-earned thanks to a ballet company and not as unequivocal testimony for scholars, these ambiguities merit no criticism. But the extent to which notations were used on this occasion has been questioned. The *affiche* of the Bolshoi Theater announced that the ballet was mounted "after dance notations made according to the Stepanov system," from which historians ever since have assumed their use. Vera Krasovskaya, however, citing an extant biography of Gorsky (whose author she does not name), writes that the notations disappeared at the first rehearsal, and that the quixotic Gorsky concealed the loss, reconstructed the work from memory, and in his address extolled the Stepanov system anyway.[26] In the absence of further evidence, it is unlikely that this point will ever be clarified.

---

[23] *Petersburg Gazette* [Peterburgskaya gazeta], 16 April 1893, p. 3, quoted from *KrasXIX*, p. 447. See also, concerning this examination, *The New Time* [Novoe vremya], 23 April 1893, p. 5, col. 3. No state documents certifying the commission's findings have been published.

[24] *Aleksandr Alekseevich Gorskii*, pp. 12-13; but Krasovskaya states that "rehearsals began 30 November 1898" (*KrasXX*, I, 114).

[25] Quoted from *KrasXX*, I, 114. In the *Moscow Gazette* [Moskovskie vedomosti], 26 January 1899, p. 4, cols. 5-6, we read: "At the Bolshoi Theater a few days ago the ballet *Sleeping Beauty* was given. This ballet, the scenes and dances of which were composed by the celebrated choreographer M. I. Petipa, was produced on the local stage according to 'choreographic notations' by artist of the Imperial Petersburg Theaters A. A. Gorsky, and, moreover, in the unprecedented period of 9 or 10 days."

[26] *KrasXX*, I, 114. The unnamed author's source is, according to Krasovskaya, a firsthand account of Gorsky's sister, Vera Alekseevna Gorskaya.

The Moscow production of *Sleeping Beauty* nevertheless provided Gorsky with an opportunity to publicize the Stepanov system, possibly in anticipation of another project: a student examination performance of his own *Clorinda* from notations, to a score compiled by Ernest Keller, flautist of the Maryinsky Theater. Like Stepanov's production of *Délire d'un peintre* in 1893, *Clorinda* was to prove the system's usefulness in the creation (as distinct from the revival) of ballets. "Having composed it in its entirety not in the rehearsal hall but at home," Soviet choreographer Fedor Lopukhov recalls, "he notated all the parts according to Stepanov's system, and distributed them to the performers. Each studied his part independently, as dramatic actors do, and it remained for Gorsky only to bring together what had been learned."[27] The examination took place 11 April 1899 at the Mikhailovsky Theater in St. Petersburg, with students who would be the pride of any school. Supporting Lyubov Petipa (Marius's daughter) as Clorinda were, among others, Anna Pavlova, Tamara Karsavina, Elsa Will, Lydia Kyaksht, Lydia Lopukhova and Fedor Lopukhov.

While the Moscow *Sleeping Beauty* may have been fortuitous—the sources refer vaguely to the theater directorate's wish to enrich the Bolshoi's repertoire—the production of *Clorinda* was planned well in advance. The dancers learned the work during the school year, and, depending on when this process began, it is possible that *Clorinda* actually predated Gorsky's work in Moscow. The *affiche* of the work claimed that it was "the first attempt to compose a ballet and its preliminary explication on paper by means of the alphabet of movements invented by V. I. Stepanov."[28]

This claim, like that Gorsky made for *Sleeping Beauty*, suggests a premeditated attempt to stimulate official enthusiasm for the notation, as Stepanov had done six years earlier with *Délire*. If this is true Gorsky's reasons can only be guessed, but it may well have been his purpose to enhance the prospect of publishing the *Table of Signs* and *Choreography:* the latter bears the date 1899, and the *Table* must certainly have been issued at about the same time. Another objective may have been to initiate the systematic notation of the Maryinsky repertoire. The choreographic records themselves contain too few dates to confirm this, but some of the most elaborate and finished notations—which would logically coincide with high ambitions at the outset of such a project—were made at the turn of the century. Those for the Petipa-Minkus *La Bayadère*, for example, were prepared on the occasion of a revival first performed in the 1900-1901 season. That this ballet and many others may have been recorded after Gorsky's transfer to Moscow does not preclude his participation in starting the administrative machinery necessary to bring the notations into being.

After the period of intensive use under Sergeyev, Stepanov notation seems to have been abandoned completely. For some of the reasons we may turn again to Fedor Lopukhov:

> "Giving him [Stepanov] all due credit, one must nevertheless say that this notation was very imperfect. This relates especially to the legato movements of the arms, wrists and fingers, which are the most expressive

---

[27] Fedor Vasil'evich Lopukhov, *Sixty Years in Ballet* [Shest'desyat let v balete] (Moscow, 1966), p. 134.

Krasovskaya provides the following description of the action of *Clorinda:* "The Tyrolean peasant Franz, at the insistence of his bride Ida, climbs up to the top of a high mountain to get an eagle's feather. Clorinda, princess of the mountain fairies, charms the youth and hurls him down a precipice. And at this moment Ida, having forgotten him, dances at a festival with a mountain spirit who is assuming a human appearance. At the end of the ballet Ida cries at Franz's grave. The mountain spirits raise up a snowstorm that brings destruction to the girl" (*KrasXX*, I, 112).

[28] *Borisoglebskii*, II, 47-48.

parts of the human body. The manifold movements of the arms, as of the turns of the head, are poorly notated by means of Stepanov's system.

The imperfection and poverty of his notation became more evident when attempts were made to record the works of Fokine and Gorsky. Both were innovators; both renewed dance. Fokine and the Legat brothers, being superb at sketching, did not accept Stepanov's system and relied more on their own drawings of poses."

Lopukhov goes on to credit Gorsky with the authorship of the *Table of Signs*, and then continues:

"In it [the *Table*] is such an innumerable number of half note signs that one would need years to become familiar with them all. A second imperfection consists of its inexactitude: the signs demand verbal clarification much more extensive than [information provided] in musical notes."[29]

Lopukhov's criticisms are valid: a method too complex yields results too imprecise. But this problem exists to some degree in all of the more comprehensive systems of movement notation, and it can be argued that Lopukhov, like Petipa (above, pp. xii-xiii) invoked clichés of criticism to divert attention from objections of a more personal kind.

One cannot take issue with Lopukhov's remark that Fokine and Gorsky, as choreographers, ignored the Stepanov notation. The true-to-life conceptions of these men remind us that the style of Russian ballet in the 1910's was developing away from classicism. It is hardly surprising that Stepanov notation, designed for recording classical steps and poses, should be thought unsuitable: it could well have been the victim of a change in choreographic taste. From a technical standpoint, this is especially probable considering the need to deal with the pantomime that figures so prominently in the works of Gorsky and Fokine. Stepanov notators recorded mime not with symbols, but in prose.

And yet another factor—an imponderable not mentioned by Lopukhov but nevertheless deserving of consideration—is the degree to which the rejection of Stepanov notation was in fact unrelated to its technical shortcomings, but was rather a rejection of Nikolai Sergeyev, who in his years of supervising the Maryinsky notation project might have become too closely identified with it for it to survive his unpopularity. To the artists Sergeyev-regisseur was a symbol of all the repressive and arbitrary attributes of tsarist officialdom. Sergeyev the teacher of notation did little to encourage acceptance of the Stepanov method, but instead (if we can judge from anecdotal reports), left his students puzzled, scornful, sometimes hostile. Thus there was no enthusiasm among the students to adapt Stepanov's method to the new trends in choreography had such adaptation been feasible technically. When one adds these objections to factors such as the new regime's antipathy toward anything with imperial trappings, Sergeyev's removal of the completed notations from Russia (leaving no sources on which to base revivals or a historical study later), and the sworn hatred for Sergeyev of Fokine, who in the late imperial days was the hope of the St. Petersburg ballet, there emerges a clearer understanding of how the system may have come to be abandoned.[30] Whatever reasons best fit the circumstances, it

---

[29] *Candid Remarks About Choreography* [Khoreograficheskie otkrovennosti], p. 53. Fokine himself writes of how, "during the production of the opera [*Orfeo ed Euridice* of Gluck] there was an attempt to notate my work according to that very system with which old ballets were recorded. But regisseur Sergeyev, having tried, gave up and said: 'what kind of dances are these, if they cannot be notated? . . .' Indeed, these dances were not similar to the old ballet, and to notate them by means of an old system was impossible." M[ikhail Mikhailovich] Fokin, *Against the Current* [Protiv techeniya] (Leningrad and Moscow, 1962), p. 503.

[30] Other reasons for Petipa's rejection of the system are similarly speculative but surely as convincing as the ones he offered officially. The possibility that they represent his irritation at

is virtually certain that Stepanov notation was no longer in use by 1920, and probably had fallen from favor some years earlier.[31]

III. Gorsky's publications.

Several accounts bear witness to the need for improvements in the system as devised by Stepanov himself, improvements attributed to Gorsky.[32] The *Table of Signs* and *Choreography* are not, then, translations of Stepanov's *Alphabet*, but revisions. (Because ballet students in St. Petersburg learned French, a mere translation would not have been necessary at the theater school.) Thus it remains to compare the *Alphabet* with Gorsky's work.

Gorsky's viewpoint differs from Stepanov's. However practical Stepanov was as a dancer and teacher, in the *Alphabet* he was an academic: the book is a learned disquisition. It begins with an *apologia* in which he reviews earlier attempts at notation. This is followed by a chapter on anatomy. The bulk of the work is an exposition of the system, without particular reference to dance, reflecting a catholic attitude confirmed by the inclusion of a chapter on gymnastics. Only in the final chapter—6 pages out of 66—does he specifically address the subject of choreography. The *Alphabet* is not unusual in assigning Terpsichore such a modest place, for it continues a tradition according to which anatomical study, the preservation of good health, or the cultivation of social graces provides the justification for treatises on dance. Considering that Stepanov's trip to Paris and his professional contact with Charcot were related to the study of anatomy, the orientation of his book is readily understood.

Gorsky, in contrast, was writing a textbook for the use of students in a ballet school. He retained a chapter on anatomy, but compared with the *Alphabet* the *Table of Signs* practically reverses the ratio of space devoted to dance and anatomy. Gorsky moves rapidly (and, as the reader will notice, somewhat carelessly) through a review of the

---

Stepanov's seeking Joseph Hansen's endorsement rather than his own has already been mentioned (above, p. xiii). Notwithstanding, his remarks on the futility of notating dances in any system whatever come from a man who, after many near-defeats in 45 years of imperial service, had achieved undisputed authority in his field and did not wish to see that authority challenged again. Fixing the choreography of any ballet would pose a threat to his option of remaking old works. And while Sergeyev could not have been a factor in Petipa's thinking when he wrote his critique in 1892, surely it is ironic that Sergeyev, whose place in the bureaucracy was nominally subordinate to Petipa's, ultimately rose to challenge the Frenchman's authority, and precisely in regard to revivals. What frustration and outrage Petipa must have experienced on occasions when Sergeyev reproduced his ballets from notations (and for additional pay) right before the old man's eyes!

[31] Two references to Stepanov notation remain to be cited in order to complete the roster of important imperial period authors who mention it. Both appear in major histories: Aleksandr Alekseevich Pleshcheev, *Our Ballet* [Nash balet], 2nd ed. (St. Petersburg, 1899), p. 414, and Sergei Nikolaevich Khudekov, *History of Dances* [Istoriya tantsev], 4 vols. (St. Petersburg/Petrograd, 1913-1918), IV, 306-307.

[32] The protocol of 1891 states that the commission declared the method extremely valuable and having "in the future" great significance for the choreographic art. A contemporary of Stepanov, the dancer Leonid Sergeyevich Leont'ev, recalled: "Stepanov's system was far from complete, but its further working-out would be to the great advantage of our choreography" (*Borisoglebskii*, II, 37). Of Gorsky's work, Lopukhov recalled: "Gorsky became interested in the [Stepanov] system and undertook to perfect it" (*Candid Remarks About Choreography*, p. 53); and elsewhere: "He [Gorsky] worked out so well the system of dance notation proposed by V. Stepanov that he astounded all those present with the ballet *Clorinda*" (*Sixty Years in Ballet*, p. 134).

The reader will notice that the title-page of the *Table of Signs* makes no reference to Gorsky, but his name appears at the end of two sections of the book, the introduction and the "Supplement to the Tables."

human skeleton, in which he stresses terms frequently used in the *Table* proper, so he can devote most of his book to practical considerations important to the dancer.

These differences in viewpoint and purpose make Gorsky's work more useful than Stepanov's for modern investigators. Perhaps because he was writing for students, Gorsky is the more comprehensive. He explains, for example, the basis of the system in the notation of positions (not movements), and elaborates on many other technical points. Gorsky provides more examples than Stepanov, and includes fully notated excerpts from *Swan Lake*, *Sleeping Beauty*, and his own *Clorinda*. In these he is concerned in part with the blocking of dancers on stage, something of which Stepanov takes no account in the *Alphabet*. Gorsky's information is, finally, more accurate than Stepanov's in relation to the practice used in the surviving notations. The *Table of Signs* gives clear explanations of certain symbols which Stepanov saw fit to omit or mention without additional comment.[33]

In fairness to Stepanov we must remember the impossibility of knowing how many of Gorsky's improvements are his own, and to what extent they relate to the continuing refinements made by the inventor before his early death, and inherited by Gorsky after his apprenticeship.

The following editorial procedures have been used in the translations:

1. Where the original was redundant, unnecessarily emphatic (bearing in mind that Gorsky was a pedagogue writing for students), or where it was desirable to break up overlong Russian sentences, idiomatic English has been given precedence over a literal reading of the Russian.

2. French words used in exercise designations have been retained; where, in the upper margins of the copy of *Choreography* used for this translation, the original omits words or symbols (due, apparently, to a mistake in cutting the pages), these have been restored by the translator.

3. The notation examples of the original edition were prepared without particular regard for legibility, and are not all complete. While photographic duplication of the original would have been desirable, it has been necessary to recopy the bulk of the non-verbal text. Editorial additions requiring new symbols have been placed within square brackets.

4. Obvious errors of spelling, etc., have been corrected: "ad lib." for "ad. lib.", "adagio" for "adajio", "più" for "piu" and the like. Similarly, errors in temporal notation, mostly concerning placement or absence of a dot, have been corrected.

5. The original authorization for publication, "Lithograph permitted by the Inspector for the Imperial St. Petersburg Theater School V. Pisnyachevsky," which, in a sixfold repetition, was spread across the bottom margins of *Choreography*, has been omitted.

6. Except as indicated otherwise, editorial footnotes are numbered. Because the *Table of Signs* and *Choreography* retain hereinafter the proportionate dimensions of the original edition, it has been necessary to collect the editorial footnotes relating to them at the end of text, before the bibliography.

---

[33] These include, for example, the notation of *pointe,* multiple body turns (as distinct from facing movements), and the signs distinguishing male from female dancers. Gorsky's *Table*, however, still does not explain all the signs used in the manuscripts, or by Gorsky himself in these publications. Only a comprehensive analysis of the choreographies will yield a complete list. The *Table* is nevertheless a much more fruitful starting place for such an analysis than the *Alphabet.* And some of the unexplained signs, such as the grace note, and "X" and "O" for man and woman respectively, need no special explanation.

IV. Acknowledgements.

It is always a pleasure for the writer to recognize in gratitude those who have contributed their kindness and expertise to his work. First, sincerest thanks are extended to Dr. Jeanne T. Newlin, Curator of the Harvard Theatre Collection, for permission to use the copy of Gorsky's treatises preserved among the Sergeyev papers, and for providing the microfilm from which the notation examples were printed. The thankless but essential task of checking the translation was graciously undertaken by Irene Kuraeff, in whom come together, mixed with patience and good humor, the talents of native speaker of Russian, lover of ballet, and professional editor. She provided a number of idiomatic alternatives to this writer's unimaginative first versions, and led him elegantly through Gorsky's labyrinthine description of the human anatomy. Ann Hutchinson Guest kindly made available for comparison a translation of Gorsky's *Table of Signs* in her possession, and responded affirmatively to numerous requests. Of the Congress on Research in Dance special thanks are due to Elizabeth Burtner, editor of *Dance Research Journal*, Patricia Rowe, editor of special publications, and to Lucy Venable, who generously consented to clarify several technical points concerning the notation and who patiently read through various drafts. Publication of the translations was supported by funds from the Horace H. Rackham Endowment of the University of Michigan at Ann Arbor and by the Capezio Foundation, to the administrators of which the translator expresses grateful appreciation.

ТАБЛИЦА ЗНАКОВЪ

для

ЗАПИСЫВАНІЯ ДВИЖЕНІЙ ЧЕЛОВѢЧЕСКАГО ТѢЛА

ПО СИСТЕМѢ

Артиста ИМПЕРАТОРСКИХЪ С.-Петербургскихъ Театровъ,

В. И. СТЕПАНОВА.

Изданіе ИМПЕРАТОРСКАГО С.-Петербургскаго Театральнаго Училища.

Harvard Theatre Collection

Table of Signs for the Notation of the Movements of the Human Body According to the System of the Artist of the Imperial St. Petersburg Theaters V. I. Stepanov. Publication of the Imperial St. Petersburg Theater School.

INTRODUCTION

Necessity for a system of notating the movements of the human body.—Attempts to find such a system.—Bases of the system of notating the movements of the human body of Mr. Stepanov.—The structure of our body; its foundation, its division into main parts and the description of the same.—Division of the movements of the human body into categories, according to the character of the movements.—Assignment of the categories of movements according to anatomical joint.—Definition of the extent of movements.—The normal position of the human body.—Aids, which serve for notating bodily movements (—Line staffs, clefs, and note signs).

The need to notate movements of the human body is especially felt in the so-called "choreographic art."

Art: painting, sculpture, architecture and music, having the propensity for graphic representation, can leave behind monuments as profound evidence of their existence and development, in the form of pictures, statues, buildings and musical scores.

That art which is made of diverse and highly complex body movements, the choreographic art, until now could not leave monuments of its existence to posterity for the absence of a means of notating these body movements.

Much that was created in the sphere of this art died with its creators. To develop, to be perfected, to move forward on a level with the other arts it could not do, because in passing from generation to generation by means of visual tradition, much was misrepresented as a result of faulty transmission, and sometimes actually for the lack of people capable of transmitting a work created by one of the masters of this art in the form it was created.

As a result of this there appeared attempts to create a system of signs for the notation of movements of the human body. In 1588 a book appeared under the title *Orchésographie,* written by Thoinot Arbeau, in which he set forth his method of notating dances. This method consists of subscribing comments under a musical note, indicating the necessary *pas.*[1] For example:

There were several successors to Thoinot Arbeau, namely Beauchamps, Favier, Desais, Feuillet, Duport, Saint-Léon and Zorn. Of these the most significant is St.-Léon, who published his system in Paris in 1852. This is an extremely well thought-out work, in which are brought together all the best thoughts of the other authors. He also wrote his signs on music staffs, but applied them rather primitively, taking each line of the staff to be a wing of the stage; the lowest line represented the first wing, the second line from the bottom the second wing, etc., and wrote signs on them.

For example:

The left leg is on the floor, the right leg lifted forward in a horizontal position.

The right leg is on the floor and bent, the left leg raised behind and bent.

The movements of the body, arms and head St.-Léon designates by the following signs:

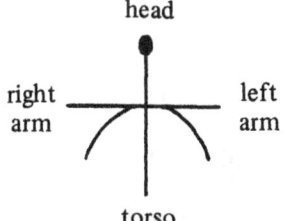

pose: attitude

Then followed the very estimable work of the Odessa teacher of ballroom dances, Mr. Zorn. In 1887 he published a book titled *Grammar of the Art of Dance* (Grammatik der Tanz-Kunst von A. Zorn. Leipzig 1887, Verlag von Weber), on which he labored more than 50 years. This work consisted of a development of St.-Léon's system. The character of the signs is purely schematic.

I give several examples from his atlas.

Separate poses

Combinations of movements

The new method of notating movements of the human body, with the aid of musical signs, belongs to the artist of the Imperial Theaters Vladimir Ivanovich Stepanov, who died in Moscow on January 16, 1896. While still a student of the Imperial St. Petersburg Theater School, he repeatedly dwelled on the thought of why human speech and sounds have means of notation, but movements did not. Developing this thought and analyzing the imagined process of the origin of an alphabet and musical notes, he conceived the idea of compiling an alphabet of movements of the human body, basing it on anatomical data under the supervision of Professor Lesgaft, and developing it in Paris under the direction of Professor Charcot. In a way similar to the sounds of music, he notated body movements by means of musical signs on a system of lines, with the aid of some supplementary signs, rhythmicizing movements just as we rhythmicize sounds.

* *
*

Before studying the signs for the notation of body movements, it is necessary to familiarize ourselves with the structure of this body, and also with the movements that can be observed in it.

At the basis of the human body is the skeleton, made up of two hundred bones of various kinds and divided into the following main parts: head (A), torso (B), upper extremities—arms (C), and lower extremities—legs (D). The head (1), by means of seven[2] cervical vertebrae (2), is joined with the torso, which consists of: a) twelve chest vertebrae (3), from which extend the ribs (4), which, arch-shaped, lead to the breastbone (5), and by means of their cartilaginous parts (6) join with it to form the rib cage; b) five lumbar vertebrae (7), which rest against the sacrum (8), which forms the posterior wall of the pelvis; the lateral walls of the latter are formed by broad iliac bones (9), the anterior wall—by the pubic bones (10).[3]

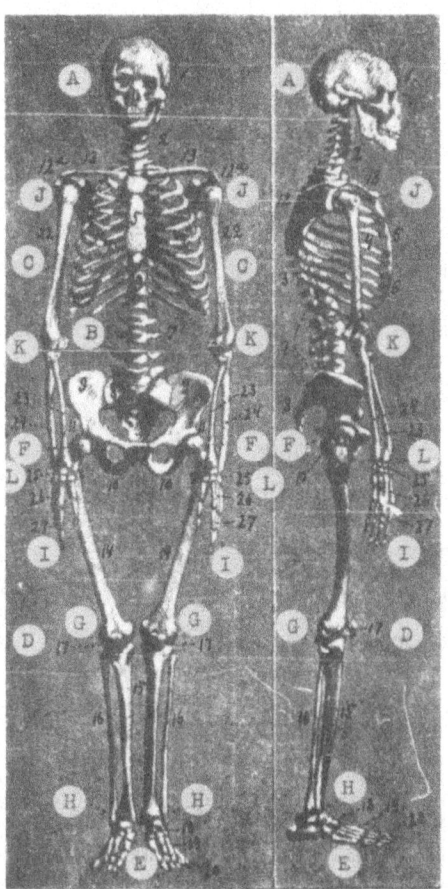

In the lower and outer parts of the iliac bones are found the cavities (11) which serve as a foundation for the lower extremities. Cervical, chest and lumbar vertebrae, connected with one another by strong but resilient ligaments, make up the spinal column. Also connected to the torso are the shoulder blades (12), joined by the appendages (12a) to the clavicles (13), which, branching off from the upper part of the breastbone and situated on the front and upper side of the torso, serve as foundation for the upper extremities.[4]

The lower extremities consist of the following parts: thighs (14), shins (15), (16) and foot (E).

The thigh consists of one thigh bone (14), which, at its upper end is joined with the pelvis, forming the hip (spherical) joint (F).

The shin consists of two bones: the tibia (15) and fibula (16). The tibia, at its upper end joined with the lower end of the thigh bone, forms the knee (pulley type) joint (G), which is covered on the front side by the knee cap (17). The fibula is attached to the exterior side of the tibia. These two bones, where joined to the foot, form the ankle joint (H).

The foot is divided into the heel (18), metatarsus (19), and toes (20). The heel consists of seven bones, the metatarsus of five and the toes (phalanges) of fourteen. The upper part of the foot is called the instep, the lower—the sole.

Consequently, in the lower extremity we observe three main joints: hip (F), knee (G), and ankle (H).

The upper extremities consist of the following parts: shoulder bone [*i.e.*, the humerus] (22), the forearm (23), (24), and hands (I).

The shoulder consists of one shoulder bone (22), which, in its upper part is joined with the thick upper end of the shoulder blade (12a), forming the shoulder (spherical) joint (J).

The forearm consists of two bones: the radius (23) on the side of the thumb and the ulna (24) on the side of the little finger. The upper ends of these bones, connected to the lower end of the shoulder bone, form the elbow (pulley type) joint (K).

The wrist consists of [eight] carpus (25), five metacarpus (26), and fourteen finger bones (phalanges) (27).

The bones of the carpus, joined with the lower parts of the ulna and radius, form the wrist joint (L). It remains to distinguish the back and palmar extremities of the wrist.

In the upper extremity we therefore see three joints: shoulder (J), elbow (K) and wrist (L).

We see that part of the bones, especially the extremities, are joined with each other by joints or articulations, that is, the ends of bones are covered by slippery cartilages, owing to the joint lubrication (mucus) on their surface, and, joined by strong (marsupial) ligaments, they permit in these parts of the skeleton various movements which are made at will through the brain and the nerves extending from it by the muscles of the body, which, fastened by tendons to the bones, produce these movements by shortening and extending like india rubber.

In notating body movements we divide the body into parts ([*i.e.,* torso/head, arms/hands, legs/feet] see *Table of Signs*, p. X). In each part we note three kinds of joints, which are divided into the joints of the body, arms, and legs, and then further divided into principal, secondary, and tertiary joints (see *Table of Signs*, p. X).

* *
*

Movements of the human body are observed, as we already said, in the joints, and are divided by type into categories of simple and complex, namely:

Simple ...	I a)—	Flexion, extension
	b)—	Adduction, abduction
	II —	Twisting movements
Complex ...	I —	Circular movements
	II —	Movements of the shoulder
	III —	Traveling movements
	IV —	Body turns

The movement flexion is observed in the following joints:

    in the hip—
        lifting the leg, forward and to the side,
    in the shoulder—
        lifting the arm forward and to the side,
    in the hip—
        bending the body forward and to the side,
    in the knee—
        flexing the knee,
    in the elbow—
        flexing the elbow,
    in the waist—
        bending the body forward and to the side,
    in the shin—
        stretching the instep,
    in the wrist—
        bending the palm to the forearm,
    in the cervical vertebrae—
        bending the head forward and to the side.

The movement extension is observed in the following joints:

    in the hip—
        lifting the leg back,
    in the shoulder—
        lifting the arm back,
    in the hip—
        extension of the body back,
    in the waist—
        extension of the body back,
    in the ankle—
        a movement back, contrary to stretching the instep,
    in the wrist—
        the bending back of the hand to the forearm,
    in the cervical vertebrae—
        the bending back of the head.

The movements adduction and abduction:

    These movements are like flexion and extension, but in between flexions [*i.e.*, they are diagonal movements]: forward and to the side, to the side and back.

The movement adduction is observed in the following joints:

    in the hip—
        a) when we lift the leg forward and adduct it almost $30°$ (the right leg to the left, the left to the right);
        b) when we lift the leg to the side and adduct it $30°$ forward;
        c) when we lift the leg to the back and adduct it $30°$ to the side;

in the shoulder—
- a) when we raise the arm forward and adduct it almost 30° (right arm to the left, the left to the right);
- b) when we raise the arm to the side and adduct it 30° forward;
- c) when we raise the arm to the back and adduct it 30° to the side;

in the ankle—
when we adduct the foot inward;

in the wrist—
when we adduct the wrist inward (toward the body).

The movement abduction is observed in the following joints:

in the hip—
- a) when we lift the leg forward and abduct it 30° to the side;
- b) when we lift the leg to the side and abduct it 30° back;
- c) when we lift the leg back and abduct it almost 30° further back (right leg to the left, left to the right).

in the shoulder—
- a) when we lift the arm forward and abduct it 30° to the side;
- b) when we lift the arm to the side and abduct it 30° to the back;
- c) when we lift the arm back and abduct it almost 30° further back (right arm to the left, left to the right).

in the ankle—
when we abduct the foot outward;

in the wrist—
when we abduct the wrist outward (away from the body).

Twisting movements we observe in the following joints:

in the hip—
turning the leg inward and outward;

in the shoulder—
turning the arm inward and outward;

in the waist—
turns of the body to the right and to the left;

in the ankle—
- a) turn of the foot inward toward the big toe,
- b) turn of the foot outward toward the little toe;

in the wrist—
turn of the hand inward and outward (the elbow remains immobile);

in the cervical vertebrae—
turns of the head to the right and left.

Circular movements are those during which some part of the human body by its extremity defines a full circle, such as, for example: a smooth movement of the head—forward, to the right, back, to the left, and forward, can be called a circular movement; a smooth movement of the leg forward, to the side, back, into normal position and forward can likewise be called a circular movement. These movements are observed in the following joints:
in the hip,
in the shoulder,
in the waist,

in the ankle,
in the wrist,
and in the cervical vertebrae.

Movements of the shoulders are the following: forward, backward, and upward.

Traveling movements are those movements during which a person makes a transition from one place to the next.

Body turns are those turns in which the body turns on its axis.

All movements in all joints are produced in circles, the centers of which are the joints in which the movements are produced.

Arcs or circles, as is well known, are measured by degrees (a degree is one 360th part of a full circle), and therefore we measure the movements of each part of the human body away from its normal position by circular motion in degrees.

Normal positions of the human body are as follows:

The legs are placed straight, heels together, toes placed outward a foot's length apart; arms freely let down along the body, wrists turned so that we see both the back side of the wrist and the thumbs at the same time; the body and head are positioned in a straight vertical line. Such a position of the human body we call normal and the basis for all body movements.

* *
*

All movements of the human body are written in notes and a few other supplementary signs, on a special system of lines, consisting of four lower, three middle and two upper lines (see *Table of Signs,* p. I).

Of these, the four lowest lines serve for the notation of foot movements, are called the staff for the notation of the movements of the feet, and are defined by a clef consisting of three vertical lines; dots around these lines indicate the place for the notation of the normal position of the feet (see *Table of Signs,* p. II).

The middle three lines serve for the notation of arm movements, are called the staff for the notation of the movements of the arm, and are defined by a clef consisting of two vertical lines; dots around these lines indicate the place for the notation of the normal position of the arms.

The upper two lines serve for the notation of the body and head, are called the staff for the notation of the body and head, and are defined by a clef consisting of one vertical line; dots around it define the place for the notation of the normal position of the body and the head.

For the notation of the principal movements (flexion and extension) in the hip joint (legs), in the shoulder joint (arms) and the hip joint (torso) the following note signs are used (see *Table of Signs*, p. I).

Note signs, as is evident, consist of two parts: a horizontal note head or dot (notes) and, extending upward or downward from it, a vertical line.

A rectangular note shows that the leg, including the complete extent of the sole of the foot, and the hand, with the complete surface of the palm, are touching the floor.

A circular note shows that the leg or arm is in the air, or is touching the floor with only the toes, or on *demi-pointe,* or with the heel (the latter is designated by additional special signs).

A vertical line extending downward from the note shows that a movement of the right leg or right arm is written by this note. A line extending upward from the note shows that a movement of the left leg or left arm is written with this note.

A vertical line extending downward and leading from the right side of the note, shows that the right leg or right arm is in front of the left.

A vertical line extending upward and leading from the right side of the note shows that the left leg or left arm is in front of the right.

A vertical line extending downward and leading from the left side of the note shows that the right leg or right arm is behind the left.

A vertical line extending upward and leading from the left side of the note shows that the left leg or left arm is behind the right.

When the heel or the wrist is in one line, as, for example, in normal (first) position, then the vertical line, extending either upward or downward from the note, always leads from the right side of the note (see *Table of Signs,* p. I).

A vertical line extending from a note that is recording a movement of the body always leads from the right side of the note and downward.

A. Gorsky

TABLE OF SIGNS

I.

for

the notation of the movements of the human body according to the system of

V. I. Stepanov.

Compiled by

Instructor of the Imperial St. Petersburg Theater School

A. Gorsky.

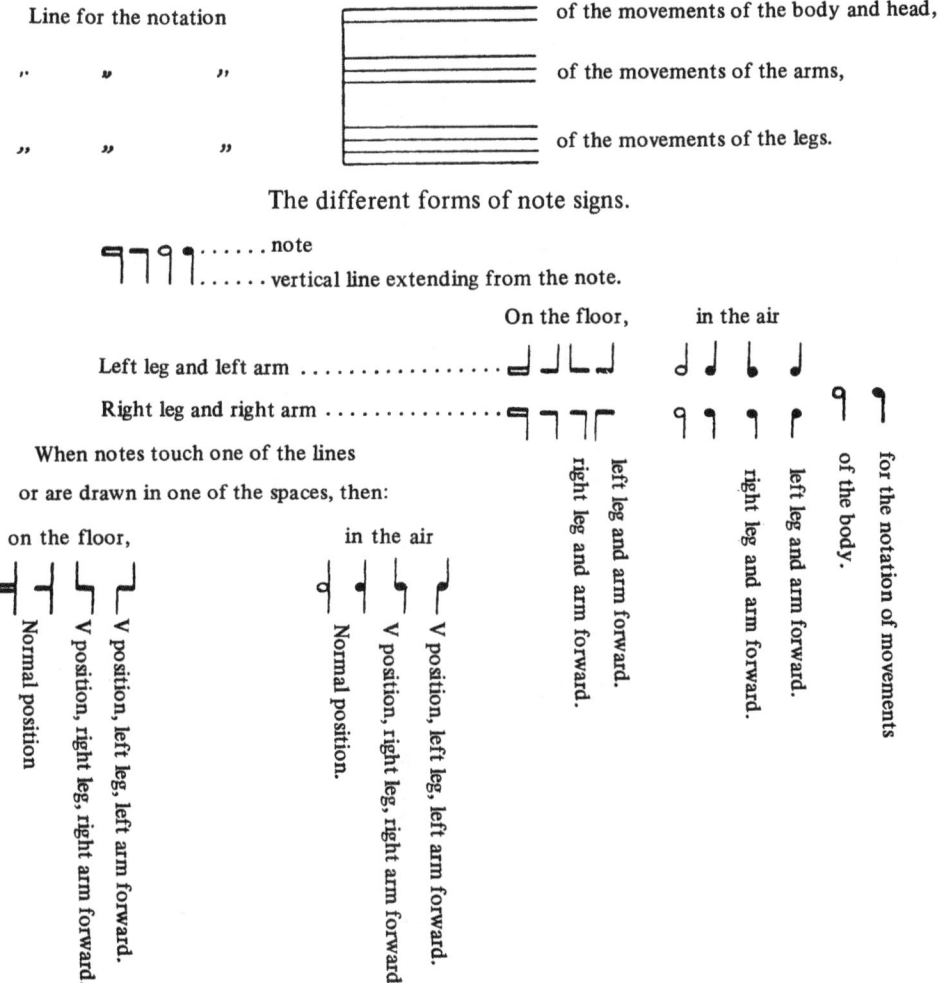

System of lines for the notation of movements of the human body.

Line for the notation ———— of the movements of the body and head,
„   „   „   of the movements of the arms,
„   „   „   of the movements of the legs.

The different forms of note signs.

...... note
...... vertical line extending from the note.

On the floor, in the air

Left leg and left arm ....
Right leg and right arm ....

When notes touch one of the lines
or are drawn in one of the spaces, then:

on the floor,   in the air

Normal position
V position, left leg, left arm forward.
V position, right leg, right arm forward.
Normal position.
V position, left leg, left arm forward.
V position, right leg, right arm forward.
left leg and arm forward.
right leg and arm forward.
left leg and arm forward.
right leg and arm forward.
for the notation of movements of the body.

[11]

II.

Clefs that define the place for recording the normal and initial position for all movements:

Clef that defines the notation of classical dances. In the clef is indicated already the turnout of the legs to the II degree throughout the whole dance.

body and head,

arms,

legs.

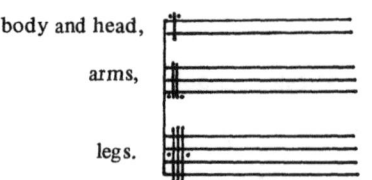
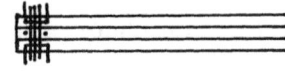

Dots in the clefs show the place for the notation of normal position.

Notation of flexion and extension:
  1) in the hip joint,
     on the floor, at 45°, at 90°, at 135°.

  2) in the shoulder joint,
     at 45°, at 90°, at 135°, at 180°.

III.

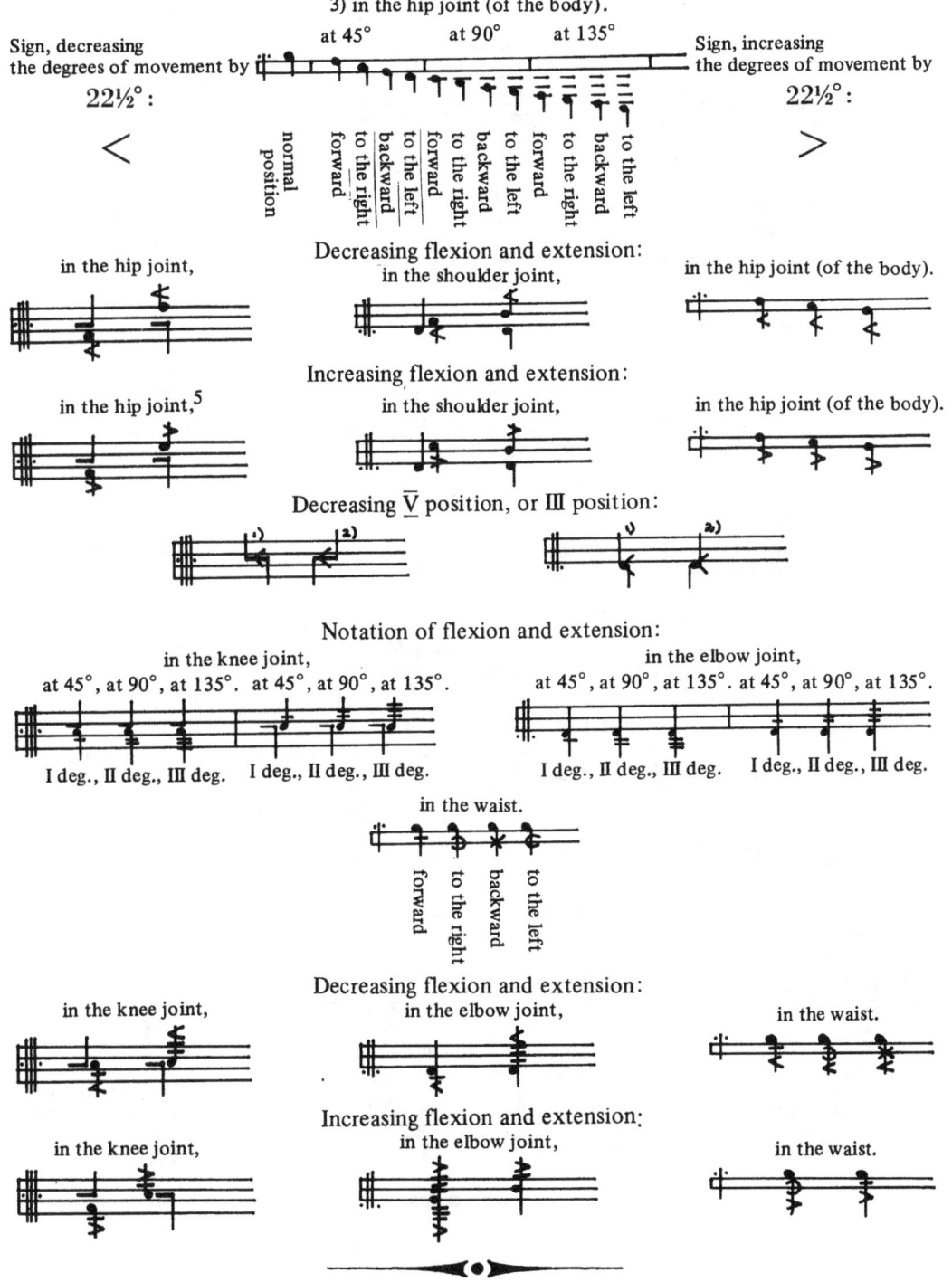

IV.

Notation of flexion:

in the ankle joint, at 45°, at 90° 
I degree　II degree

in the wrist joint, at 45°, at 90° 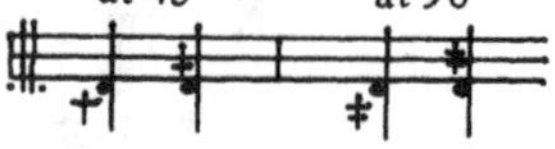
I degree　II degree

in the cervical vertebrae. 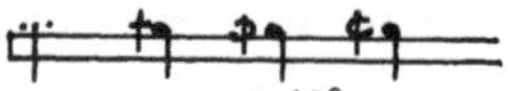
at 45°　forward　right　left

Notation of extension:

in the ankle joint, at 45° 
I degree

in the wrist joint, at 45° 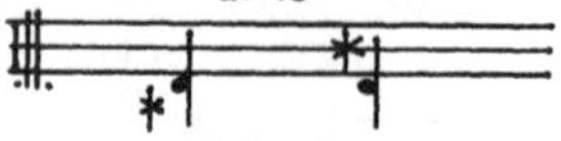
I degree

in the cervical vertebrae. 
at 45°　back

Decreasing flexion and extension:

in the ankle joint,

in the wrist joint,

in the cervical vertebrae.

Increasing flexion and extension:

in the ankle joint,

in the wrist joint,

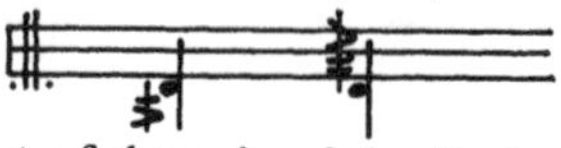

in the cervical vertebrae.

Signs of contact of the sole of the foot with the floor:

demi-pointe 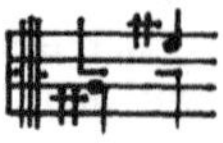　pointe 　heel 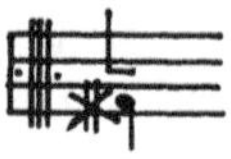　or

Notation of adduction and abduction:

in the hip joint,　in the shoulder joint,　in the ankle joint,　in the wrist joint.

Adduction

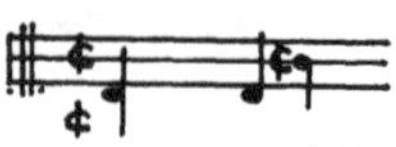

Abduction

Decreasing adduction and abduction:

in the hip joint,　in the shoulder joint, 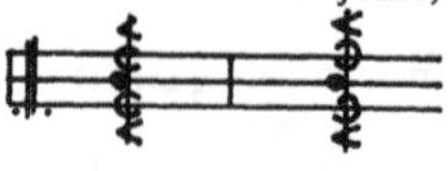　in the ankle joint, 　in the wrist joint.

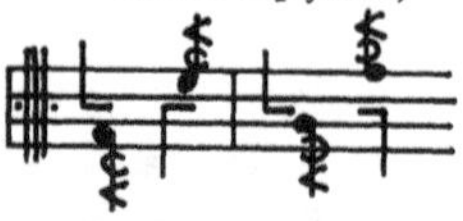

Increasing adduction and abduction:

in the hip joint,　in the shoulder joint, 　in the ankle joint, 　in the wrist joint.

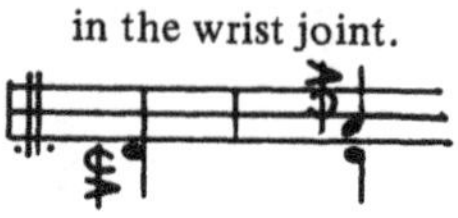

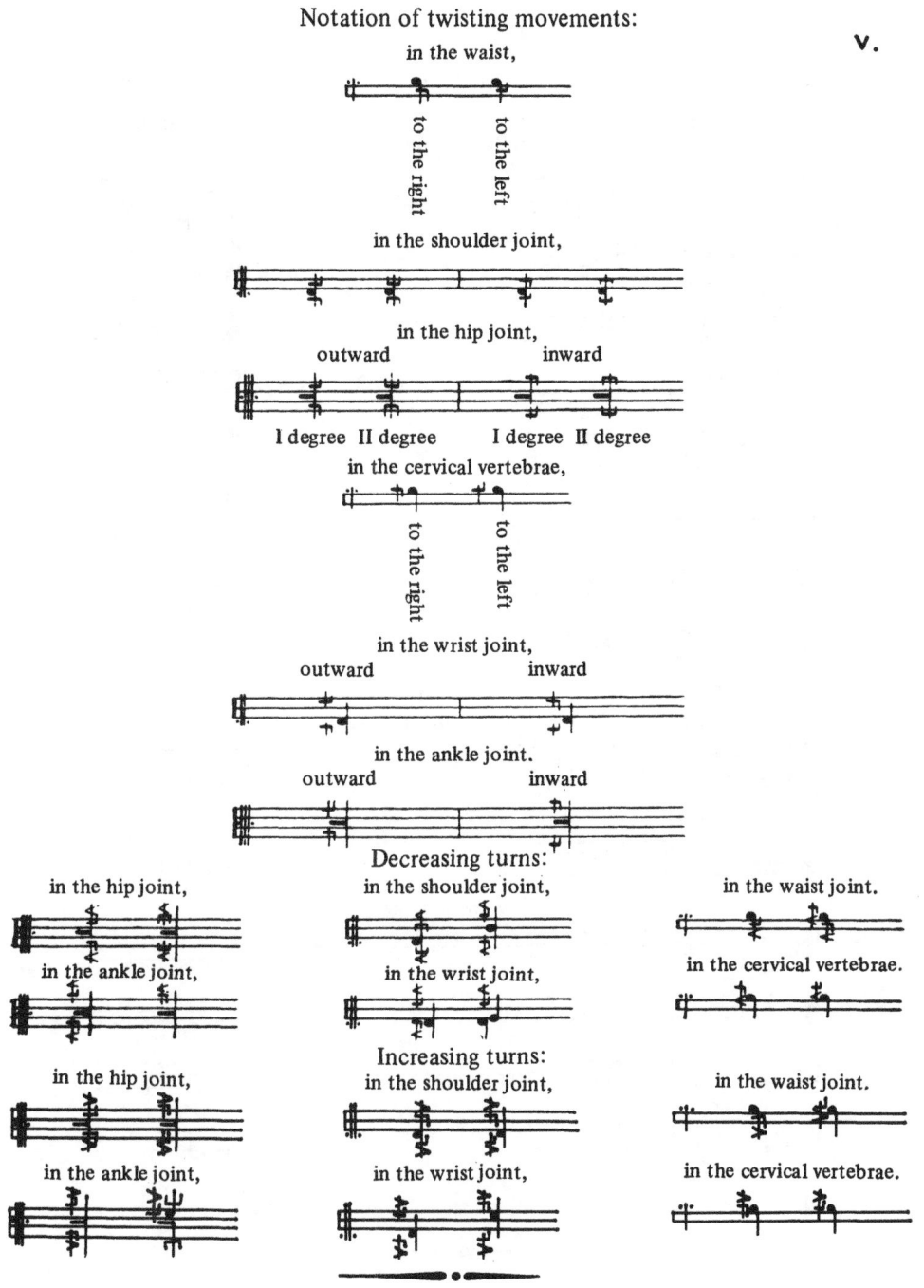

VI.

Notation of circular movements:[6]

As performed: As notated:

in the hip joint,[7]

[8]

[9]

[10]

[11]

en dehors — Notation of Ronds de jambe:[12] — en dehors

en dedans   en dedans

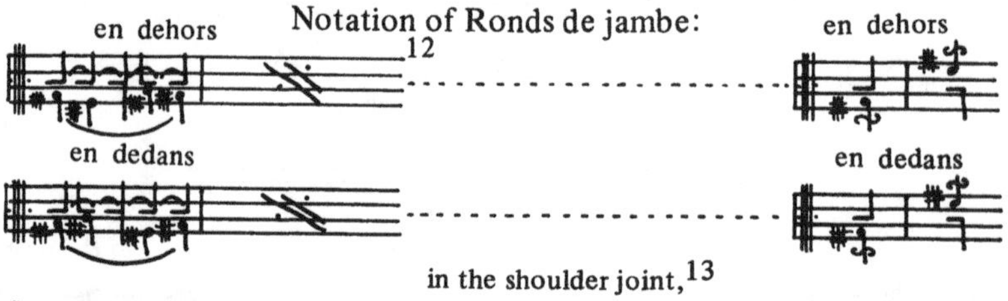

in the shoulder joint,[13]

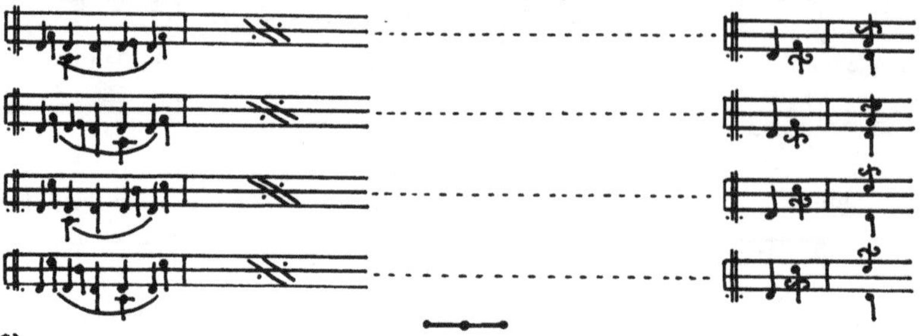

*)  — sign indicating repetition of the same, but on the other leg

VII.

As performed: As notated:

in the shoulder joint,[14]

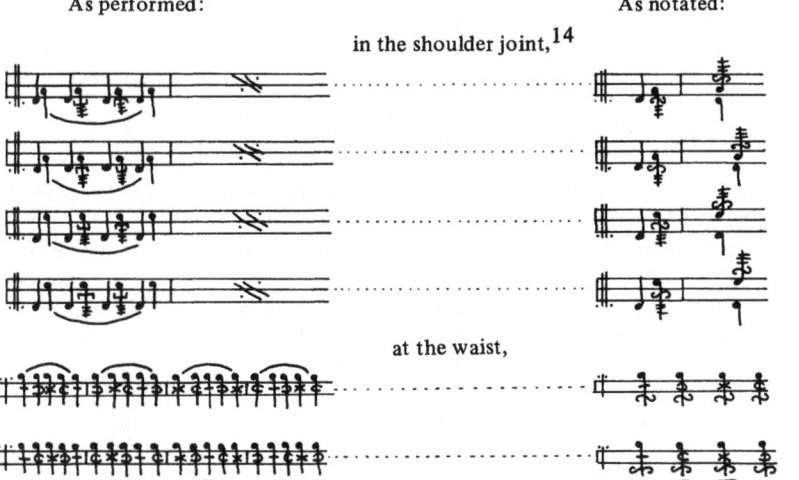

at the waist,

in the cervical vertebrae:

Exactly the same as in the waist, except that signs are placed on vertical lines next to the note symbols where movements of the head are notated.

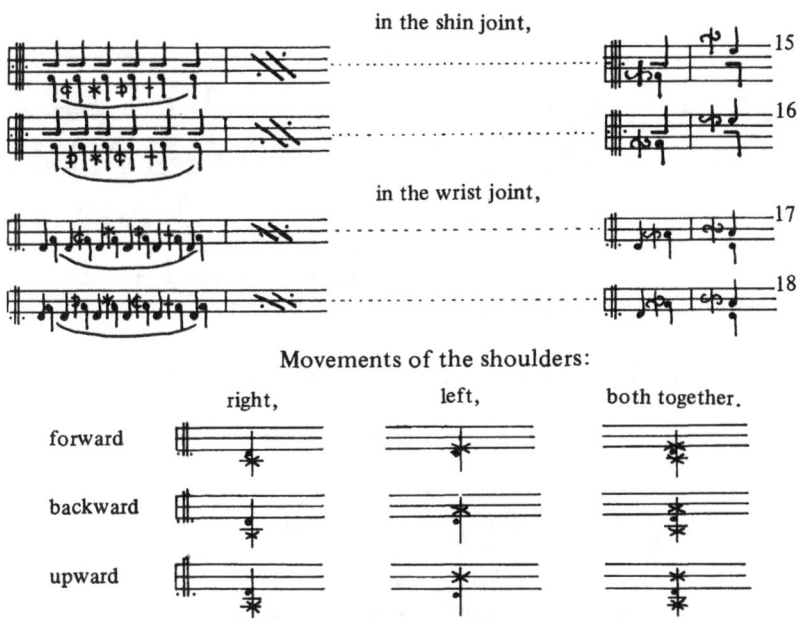

in the shin joint,

in the wrist joint,

Movements of the shoulders:

[17]

Traveling movements:

VIII.

Those movements are called traveling movements during which a person moves from one place to another; the notation of these movements is as follows:

forward,   to the right,   backward.

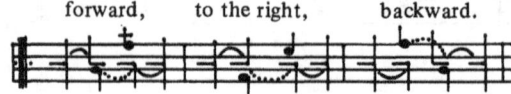

A dotted arch indicates that the leg moves down to the floor in the same place as over which it had been raised.

A small arch that connects two successive notes indicates the unchanging position of the legs, arms or body.

A large arch that connects or, so to speak, that embraces (see the circular movements) several notes indicates smoothness, the continuity of movements.

The rhythm of signs.

Movements are divided into beats:

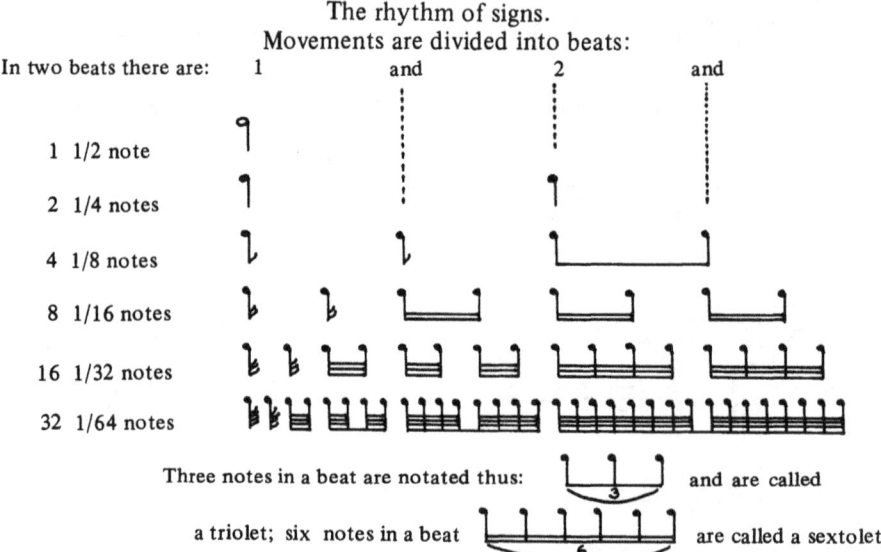

Three notes in a beat are notated thus: [figure] and are called a triolet; six notes in a beat [figure] are called a sextolet, five a quintolet and so forth.

The relative duration of the beats is defined, as in music, by words.

Here are the most used terms:

Adagio = slow
Moderato = moderate
Allegro = rather fast
Vivo = lively
Presto = fast

These words are written in above the uppermost line (the body clef).

Beats are divided into parts (or measures) by 2's, by 3's, by 4's and more beats in each. The first beat of each part must be strong, the remainder weak.

The number of beats in a part is designated by a fraction immediately following the clefs,

for example:

A dot to the right of the note adds to it one half its value.
Nuances of execution are set forth in words, which may be found in any music grammar.

Turns.

Turns are notated by means of small numbers, which are distributed around a circle in the following order:

public (audience)

These numbers are placed between the lines for the notation
of the movements of the legs and arms.
A full turn to the right is designated by the sign +
A full turn to the left is designated by the sign −
Several full turns are designated thus: $+^2$, i.e.,
two turns to the right, $-^3$, i.e., three turns to the left.
Numbers are joined by a dotted line
when the turn is to be completed smoothly, for example: 0 . . . 1 . . . 2 . . . 3

Groups and the movements of masses are designated on the floor plan in the following manner:

Group: Movement:

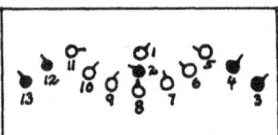 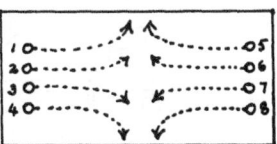

A woman is designated by the sign ♀, a man by the sign ♂.

Division of the h[uman] b[ody] into three parts: X.
1) torso and head, 2) arms, 3) legs.

Division of the joints into:

Joints of the	Principal	Secondary	Tertiary
torso	hip	lumbar vertebrae	cervical vertebrae
arms	shoulder	elbow	wrist
legs	hip	knee	ankle

Division of movements into categories:

Simple: I a) Flexion, extension
            b) Adduction, abduction
       II) Twisting movements

Complex: I Circular movements
              II Movements of the shoulders
              III Traveling movements
              IV Turns [of the entire body]

Table illustrating schematically move[ments] of adduction and abduction in the waist and shoulder joints:

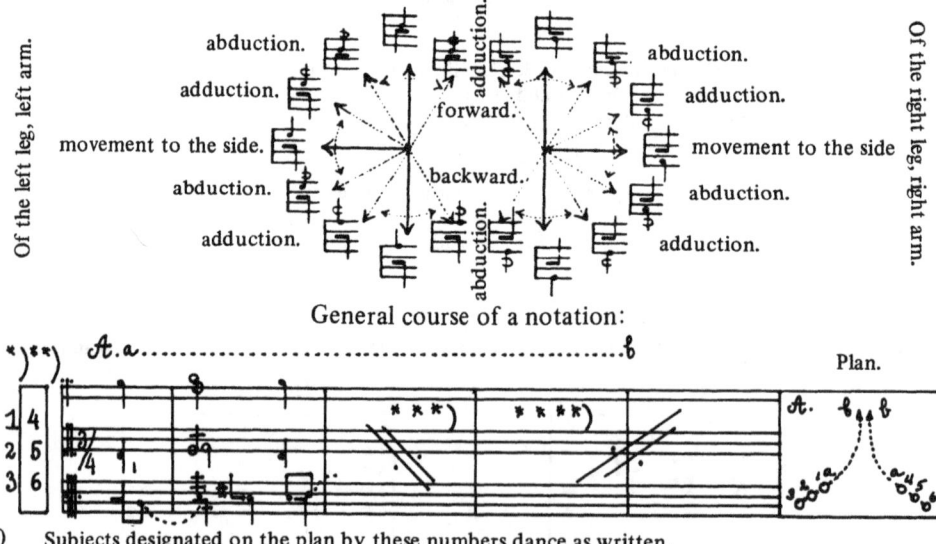

General course of a notation:

*)   Subjects designated on the plan by these numbers dance as written.
**)   Subjects designated on the plan in the square dance on the other leg or to the other side.
***)   Sign indicating repetition of the preceding measure, but on the other leg.
****) Sign indicating repetition of the two preceding measures.

END.

SUPPLEMENT TO THE TABLES

About the clef for the notation of classical dances.

The clef that is used in notating classical dances, besides indicating that the legs are turned out at all times [see *Table of Signs,* p. II], simplifies the notation of several positions of the legs, for example:

poses, notated on the ordinary clef:

are notated thus on the clef of classical dances:

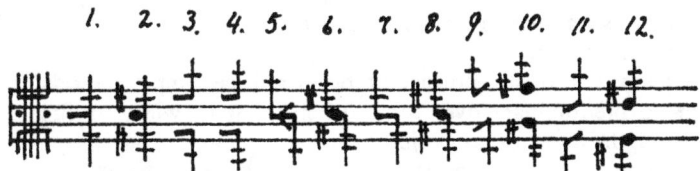

About the rhythm of movement.

Before speaking about the rhythm of movement, that is, about the relative duration of poses and movements, it is necessary to explain the following: strictly speaking, we do not notate the movements of the human body; we notate precisely only the poses, that is, the extreme points of each given movement. Taking into account that movements are produced from point to point in a straight line, we in our notating must show exactly every deviation from this straight line; then we must turn our attention to what kind of character the transition from one point to the next has, that is, whether it will be a fast little jump or a smooth, gradual transition.

We know that each pose, each movement lasts a certain amount of time. This length is measured in arbitrary although equal segments of time. Taking each such segment as "one" or one time unit, we express it with a quarter note sign (see *Table of Signs,* p. VIII). This sign we call the quarter, the poses or movements which last one time unit we notate with these signs. Poses or movements lasting two units of time we notate with signs called halves (1/2), as they are made up of two quarters.

Poses or movements lasting three units of time are expressed with half note signs, with a dot to the right of the note. A dot to the right of a note adds to the note one half its value, in this case, the value of a quarter to a half.

Poses or movements lasting four units of time are notated with two half notes connected by arches.

Poses or movements lasting only half a time unit are expressed by eighth note signs.

Poses or movements lasting one fourth a time unit are expressed by sixteenth note signs, and so forth.

On page VIII of our *Table of Signs* we note that movements produced within a given time period can be combined into a group of signs, which is perceivable as a single unit because the signs are joined together.

During the notation of movements, we must strictly observe this combination and group the signs such that, at first glance, is clearly seen not only the unit of time, but also its parts, especially the second half of each beat (which we will indicate with the word "and" [or the symbol "↕"]).

We notate in this way non-rhythmic movements, measuring them only in relation to each other.

In the notation of rhythmic movements such as gymnastic exercises and dances, we must divide our units into periods (parts).

The reason for this is that we call "rhythmic movements" such movements as have strong and weak beats. The latter, regularly alternating between themselves, constitute equal periods or measures. The measure or the period always begins with a strong beat, and ends with a weak beat before the following strong.

Periods can be in duple time or triple time, simple and complex.

Simple duple periods ordinarily are made up of two units of time, that is, quarters.

Simple triple periods can be made up of three units of time, that is, quarters, and also of three half-units, that is, of three eighths.

One period is separated from another after it by a vertical line, which is drawn across the entire clef system.

Complex periods normally consist of two or three simple periods when one of the periods appears to predominate over some others, that is, when its first beat is stronger than the first strong beats of other periods.

If in some one of the periods three poses are assigned to one of the units of time, then they are notated by means of three eighth note signs joined together, and above (or below) the line that connects these three signs is placed a small ligature (arch), and between the line and arch the number 3; such a grouping of signs is called a triolet or triplet.

If three such poses are assigned to one eighth (half a time unit), then they are notated as sixteenth note signs.

One can also have quintolets, sixtolets and so forth, that is, groups consisting of signs of five, six, and so forth. The latter are notated already by means of sixteenth and thirty-second note signs and also, like the triplet, are defined by a small number 5, 6, and so forth.

In the notating of rhythmic movements we must indicate, immediately after the clef, in the middle of the clef system, the number of units or the number of parts of units (eighths) included in the period. This number is indicated by a fraction, such as: 4/4, 2/4, 3/4, 3/8, 2/2, 6/8, 5/4, 7/4.

In the notation of movements that are accompanied by music, we must always coordinate the periods with the musical measures.

The first beat of the period must always fall, so to speak, on the leg with the first beat of the musical measure.

The number of time units (quarters) in the period must be the same as in the musical measure.[19]

Let us remember that at the beginning of this chapter we said that movements can proceed by jumps (holding the pose) or smoothly; in the first instance the signs are not connected with each other, but in the second instance those movements that proceed smoothly (gradually making the transition from one indicated pose to the next) are connected by a common arch, called a ligature.

The extent of the time unit, that is, its greater or lesser duration, is defined in exactly the same way as it is for music—by means of words. We will set forth here the terms most often used:

Those defining slow movements:
    Adagio—quite slowly
    Lento—slowly
    Andante—calmly
    Moderato—Moderately
    Allegro moderato—lively
    Allegro—gaily, quickly

Those defining fast movements:
    Allegro con brio—loudly, gaily
    Allegro assai—very gaily
    Allegro vivace—fast
    Presto—very fast
    Prestissimo—as fast as possible

The character of any given movement is defined, as in music, either by words or by signs.

Abrupt movements, that is to say, movements with strong accents, are defined by the following sign >; this little sign is placed, for the right leg, right foot and the body above the note, and for the left leg and left arm below the note. Movements that follow one another abruptly, staccato, are defined by little dots, which are placed in the same location as the preceding accent signs.

                            A. Gorsky

Harvard Theatre Collection

A. Gorsky, *Choreography; Examples for Reading*. Publication of the Imperial St. Petersburg Theater School. Installment I, 1899.

I
SIMPLE MOVEMENTS

Flexion and extension in the hip and shoulder joints.

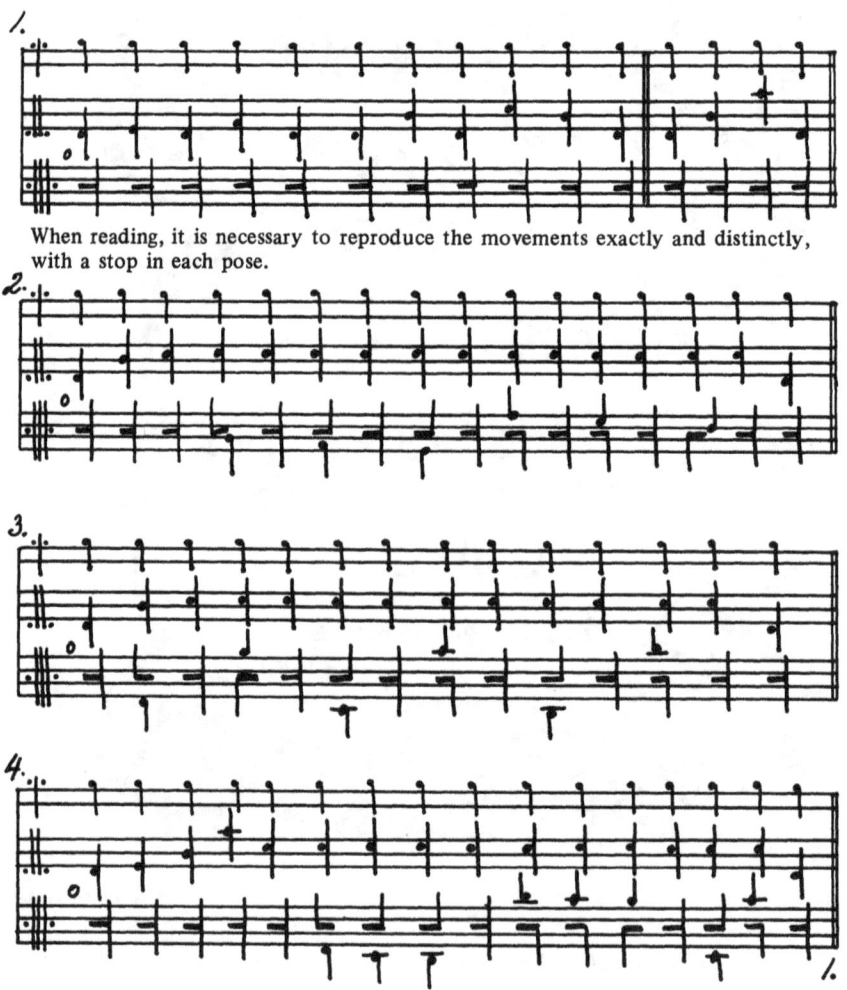

When reading, it is necessary to reproduce the movements exactly and distinctly, with a stop in each pose.

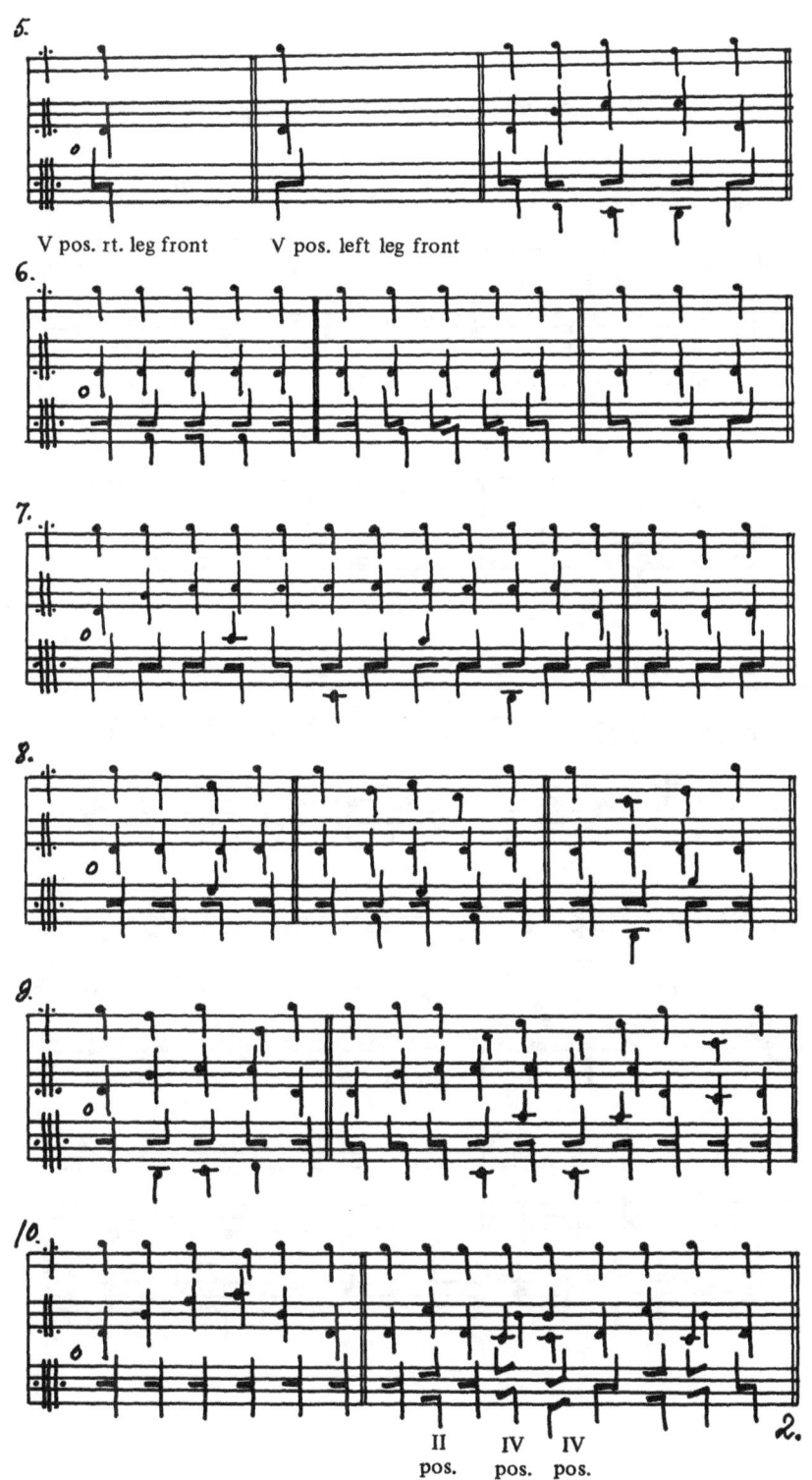

Flexion in the elbow and knee joints.

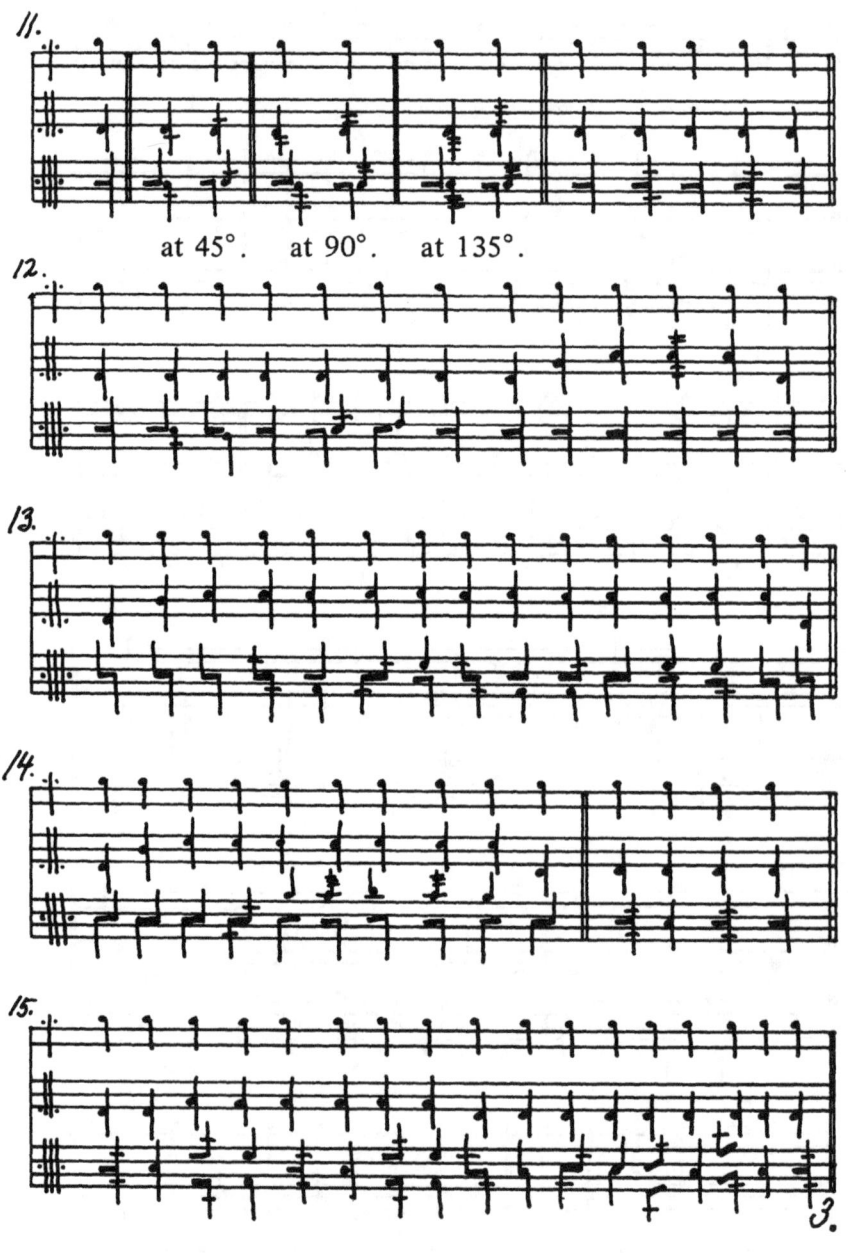

Signs that are joined, as shown above, by a horizontal bar, show us that in the time of one movement, written as an unjoined sign, come two movements written with signs joined together. We call the separate, unjoined signs "quarters," and those connected in pairs or greater numbers by one horizontal bar "eighths."

Flexion and extension at the waist.

— Sign of flexion forward, ⊃ —to the right, ✗ —back, ⊂ —to the left.

[30]

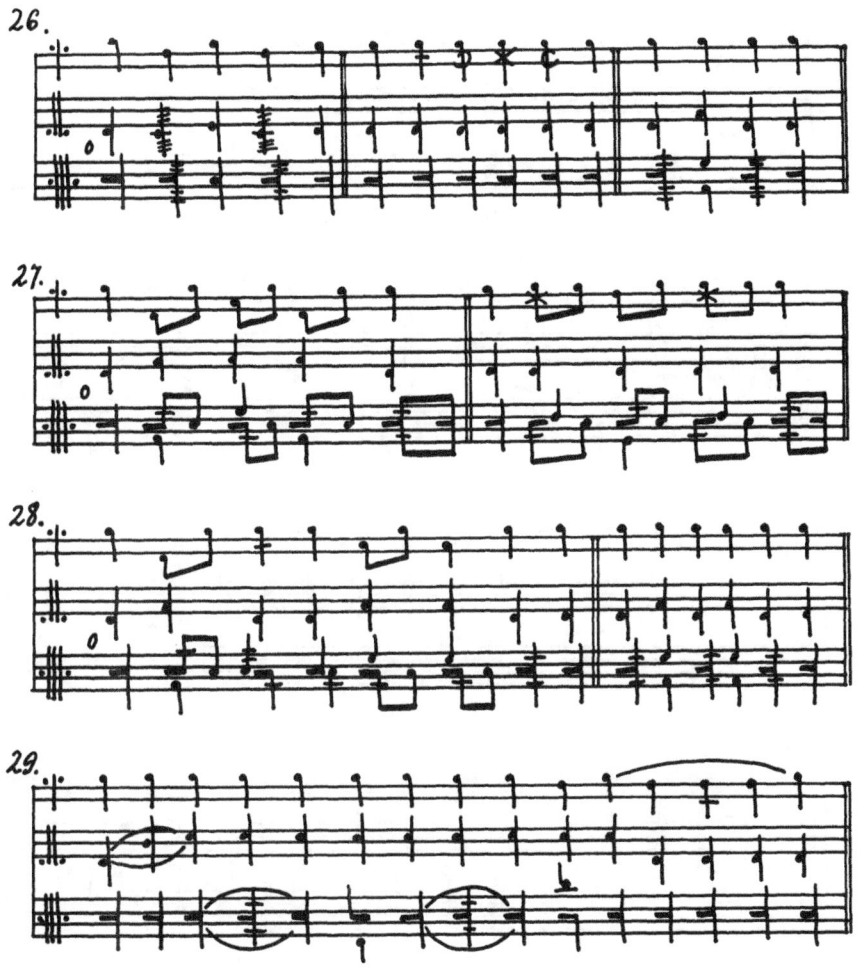

Arches connecting several poses, as shown above, show us that the movements between these poses must be performed smoothly, without breaks or accents.

Adduction and abduction in the hip and shoulder joints.

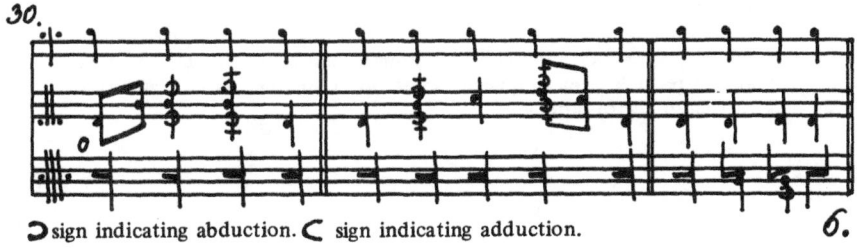

⊃ sign indicating abduction. ⊂ sign indicating adduction.

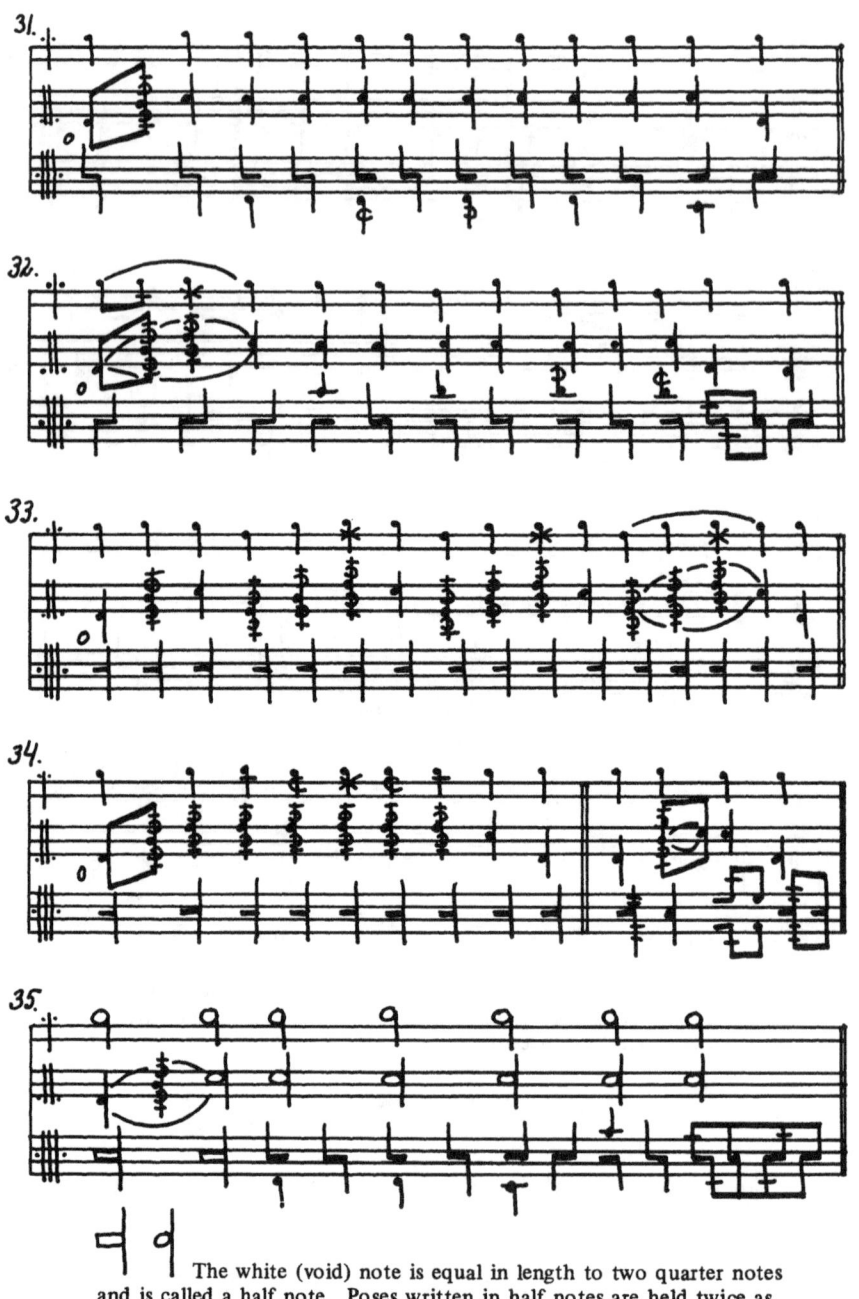

The white (void) note is equal in length to two quarter notes and is called a half note. Poses written in half notes are held twice as long as poses written in quarter notes, and four times as long as poses written in eighth notes.

7.

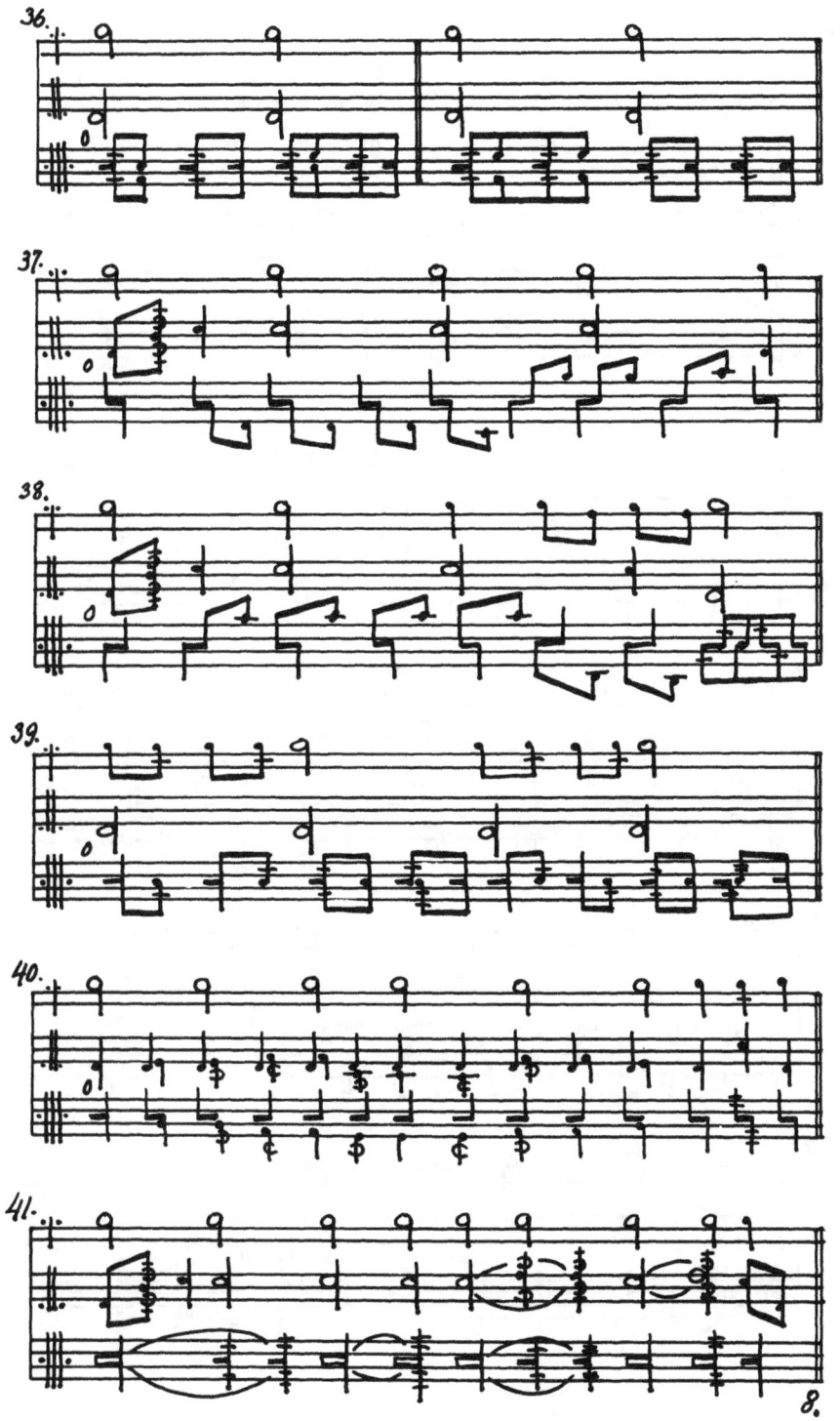

Twisting Movements

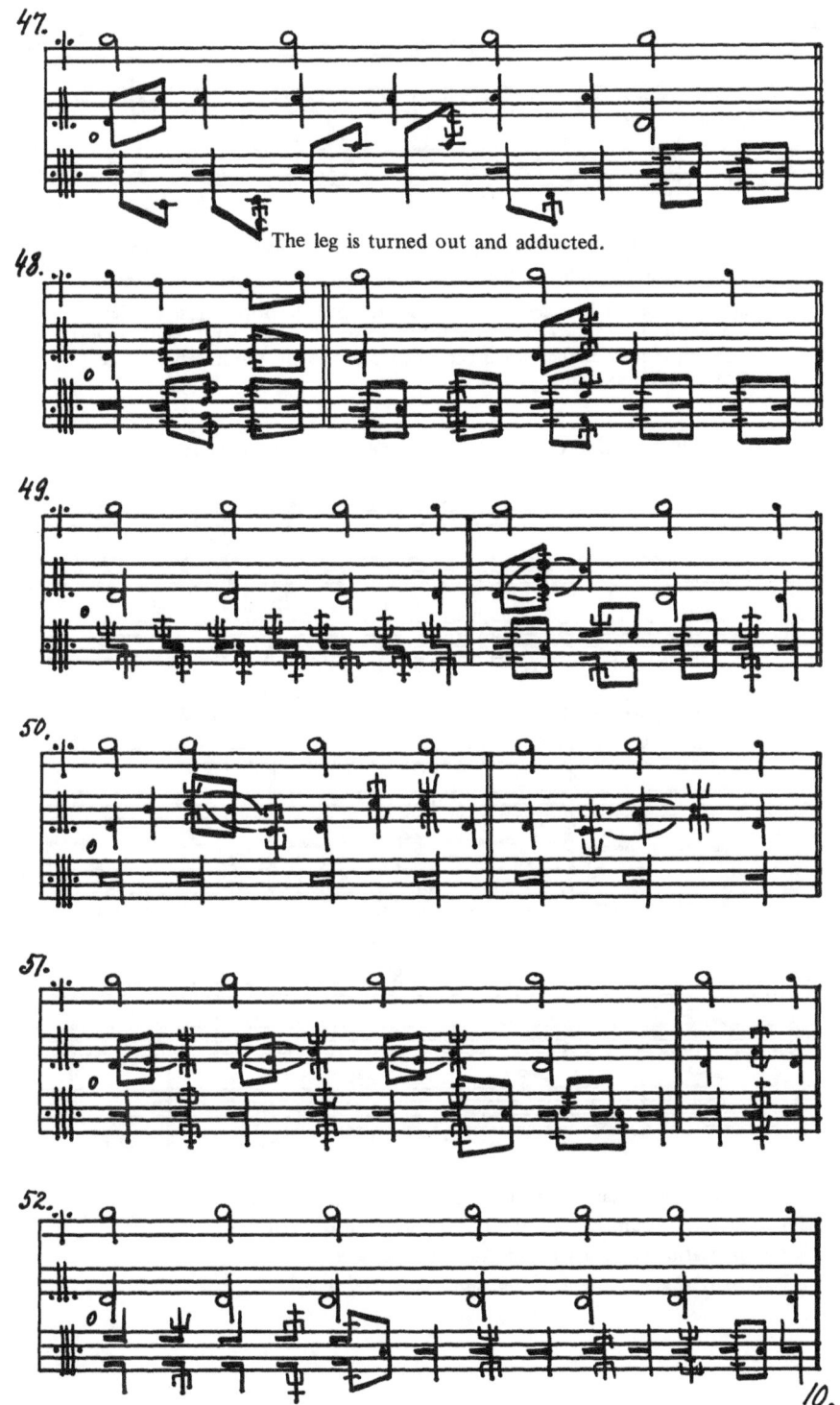

The leg is turned out and adducted.

The sign indicating the turning outward to the II degree, which is written into the clef ⧉, tells us that we must make all poses and movements notated after such a clef with turned out legs henceforth until another change in clef. This clef is called "the classical dance clef," and, besides turnout, it tells us that when the legs are in the air, the instep and the toes must be extended.

Flexion and extension: the foot, wrist, and head.

╫ sign indicating contact with the floor, demi-pointe; only the instep extended
╫ sign indicating contact with the floor, pointe; instep and toes extended
✳ sign indicating contact with the floor of the heel
✣ sign indicating extension of the foot, wrist, and head.

[37]

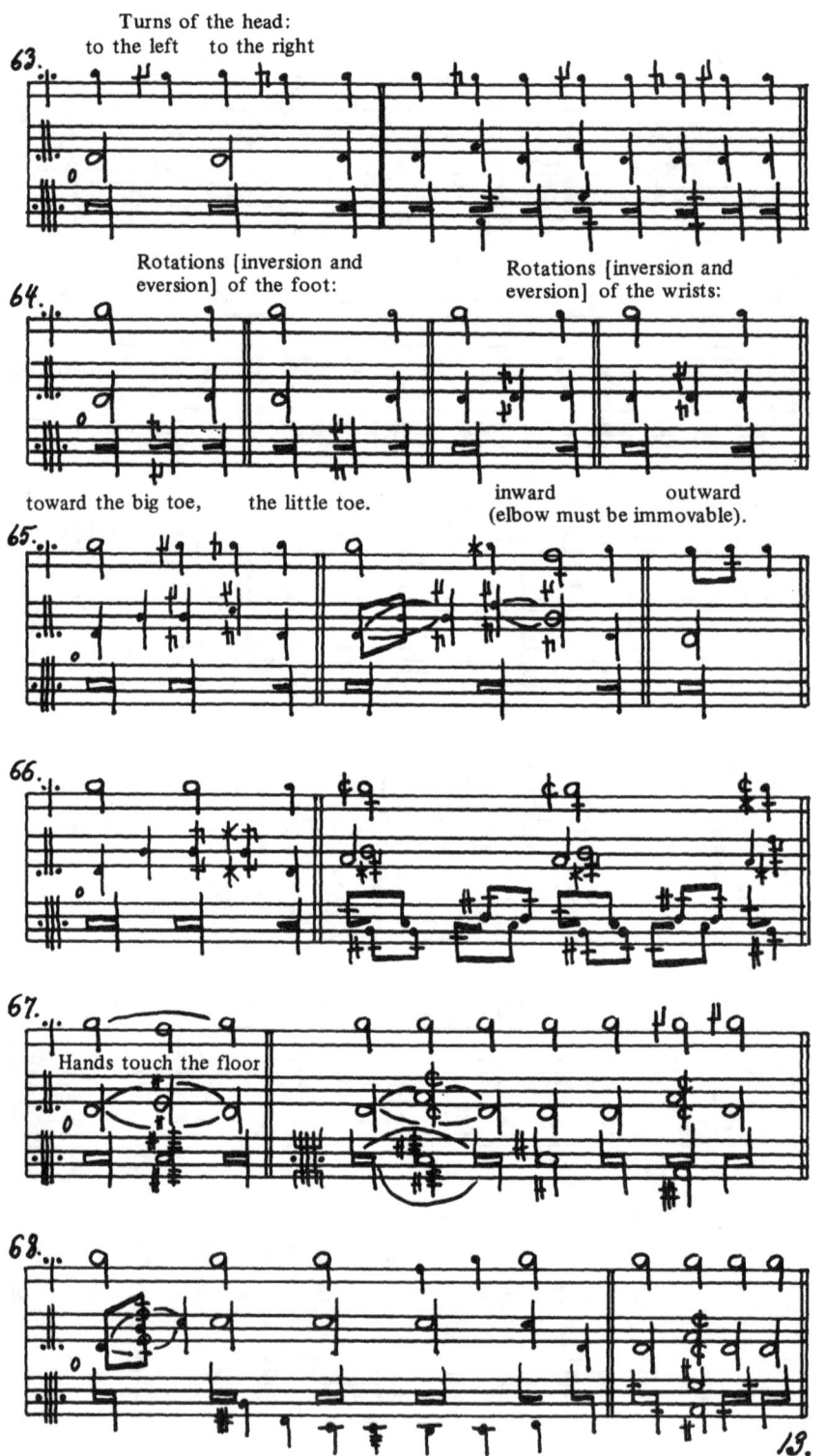

A dotted arch between notes shows that, in moving from one pose into another we also move from one place into another. We perform this transition in the direction of the raised leg, which is responsible for making the transition.

II
COMPLEX, RHYTHMICIZED MOVEMENTS

In studying the preceding examples, we produced movements evenly, interpreting the duration of the pose notated in quarter notes to be approximately two seconds. If a pose were notated with an eighth note, one second. If the notes were not connected by an arch, we would make a transition from one pose into the next quickly, but if the notes were connected with an arch, we would make the transition smoothly, gradually.

Producing the exercises with elementary examples, we counted off our quarters thus:

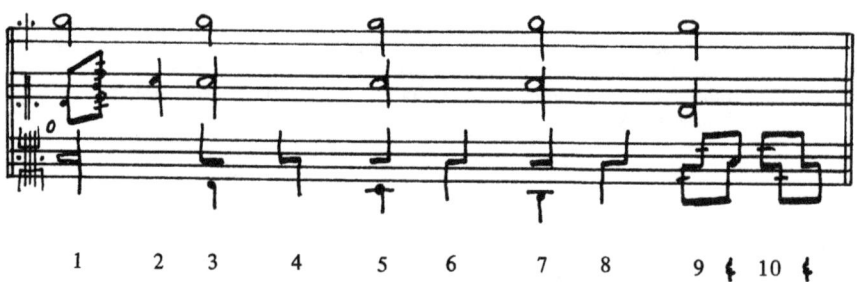

But take an example not of 9-10 positions (as above), but of a hundred: obviously, it will be necessary for us somewhere to start our count from the beginning, *i.e.*, from "one", and it is precisely for this reason that a certain equal number of quarters or notes of another value (but together equalling a set amount of quarters) are separated from one another by a vertical line crossing the entire clef system. In this instance, after each such line, which is called a barline, we start our reckoning from the beginning, that is, from "one." For example:

15.

In each measure, that is, in the space between the barlines, there may be two, four, or three quarters, three, six, or nine eighths, or other combinations, but in each separate measure the number of quarters or eighths must be identical. The number of such time units in each measure is indicated by a fraction, which is placed immediately after the clef in the middle of the clef brace. In the example given above the fraction 2/4 shows us that in each measure there must be—no more and no less than—two quarters or a value equivalent to them: one half, or four eighths, or eight sixteenth notes.

Classical Dances.

a. Beginning Exercises.

*) Sign indicating repetition of the two preceding measures, but with the other leg.

**) A dot to the right of a note adds to that note one half of its duration, that is, to a half note an additional quarter note's value, to a quarter note an additional eighth, to an eighth, an additional sixteenth, etc.

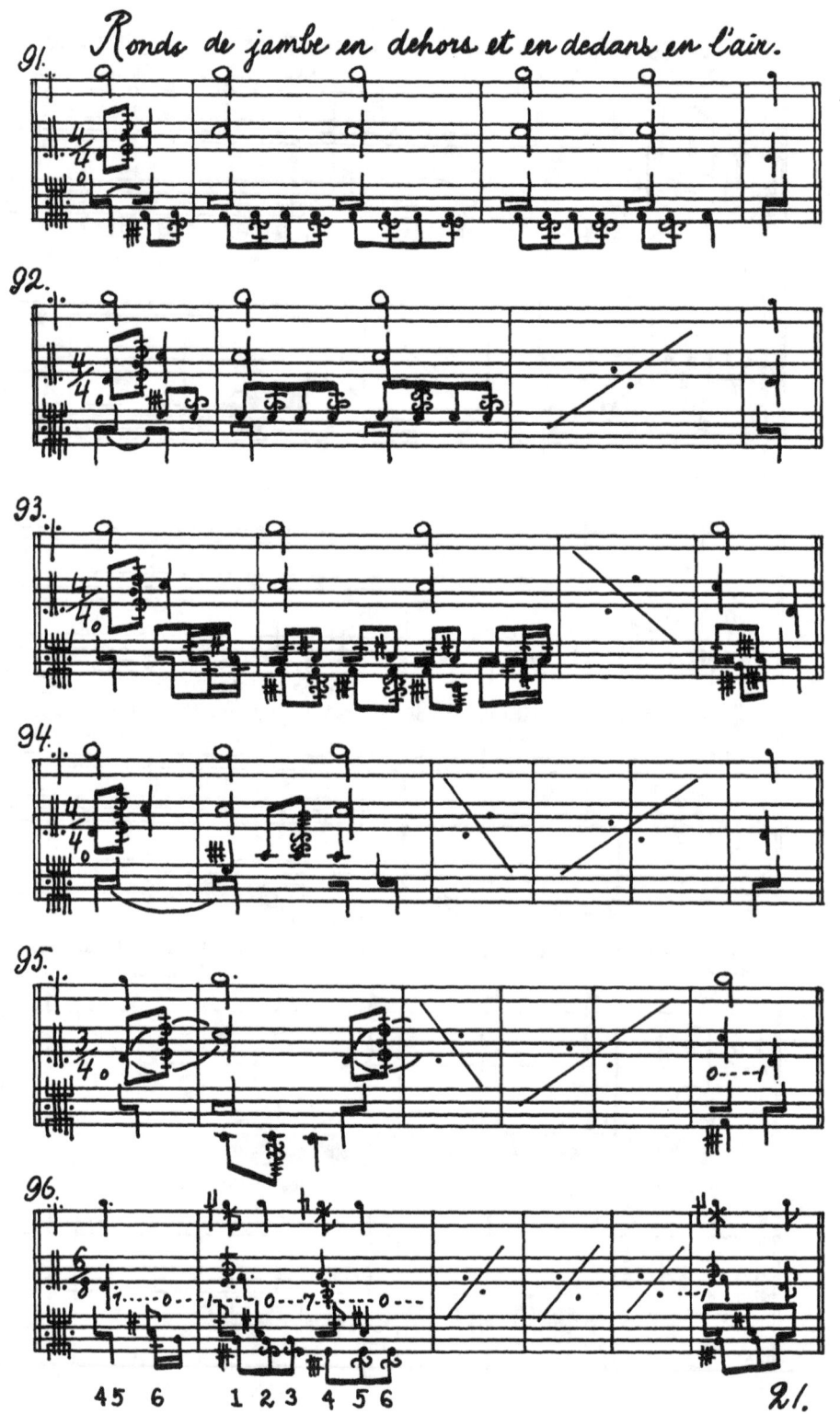

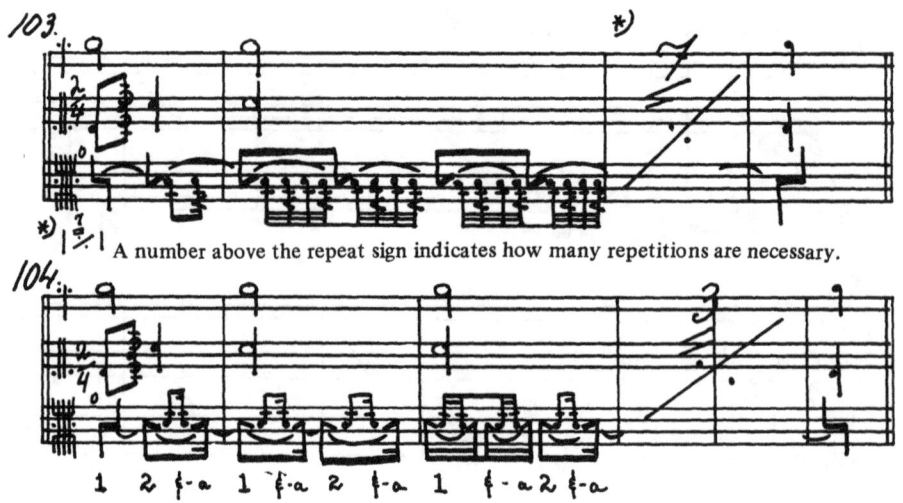

*) |%| A number above the repeat sign indicates how many repetitions are necessary.

b. Slow dances. Adagio.

*) Sign indicating repetition of the four preceding measures on the other leg.

The sign (+) designates a full turn to the right; the sign (-) a full turn to the left.

b. Fast dances. (Jumps)

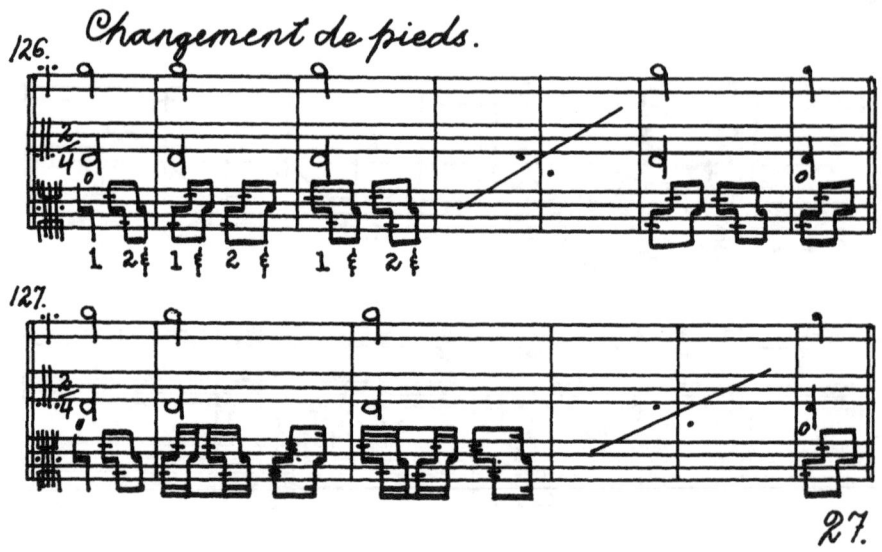

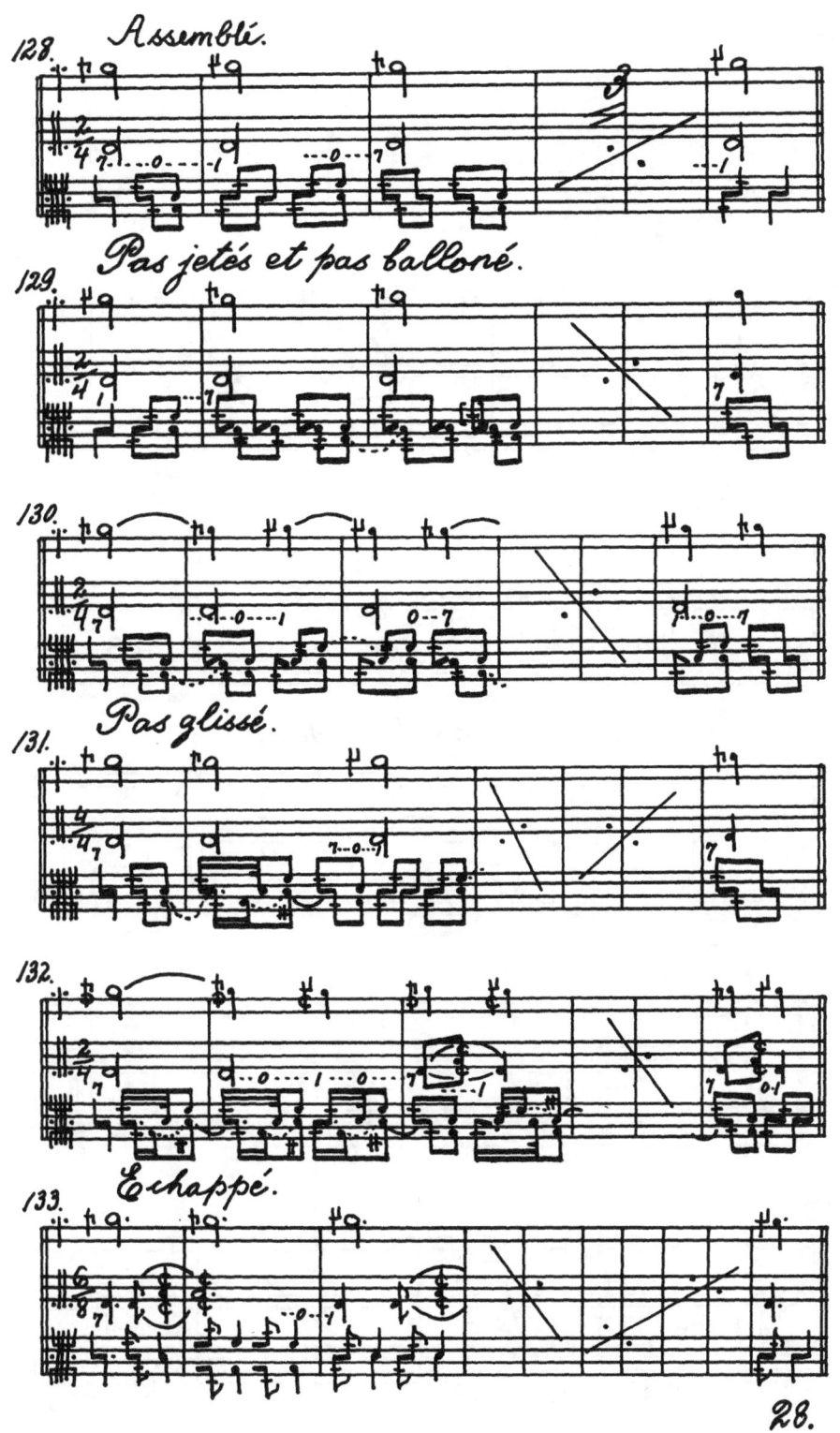

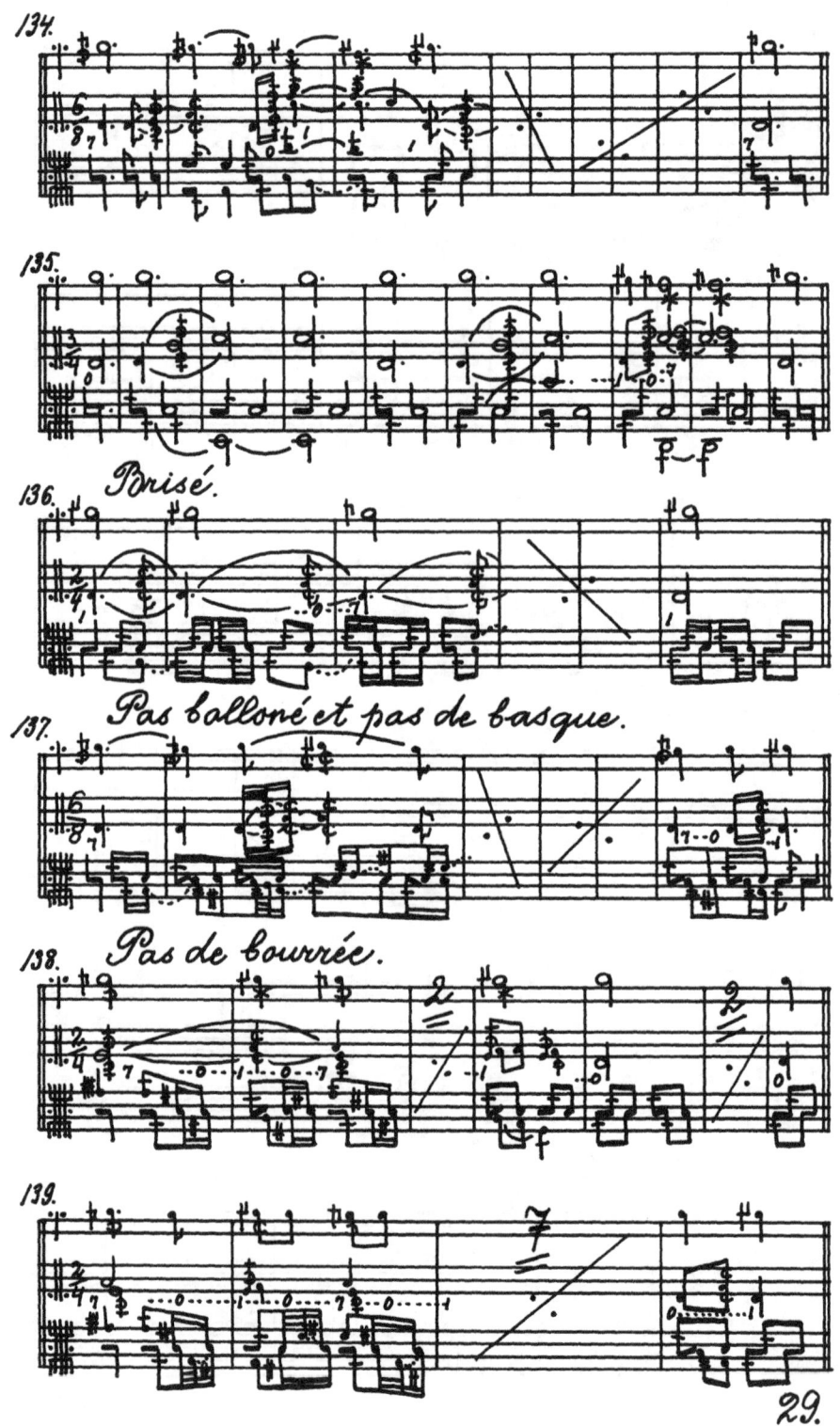

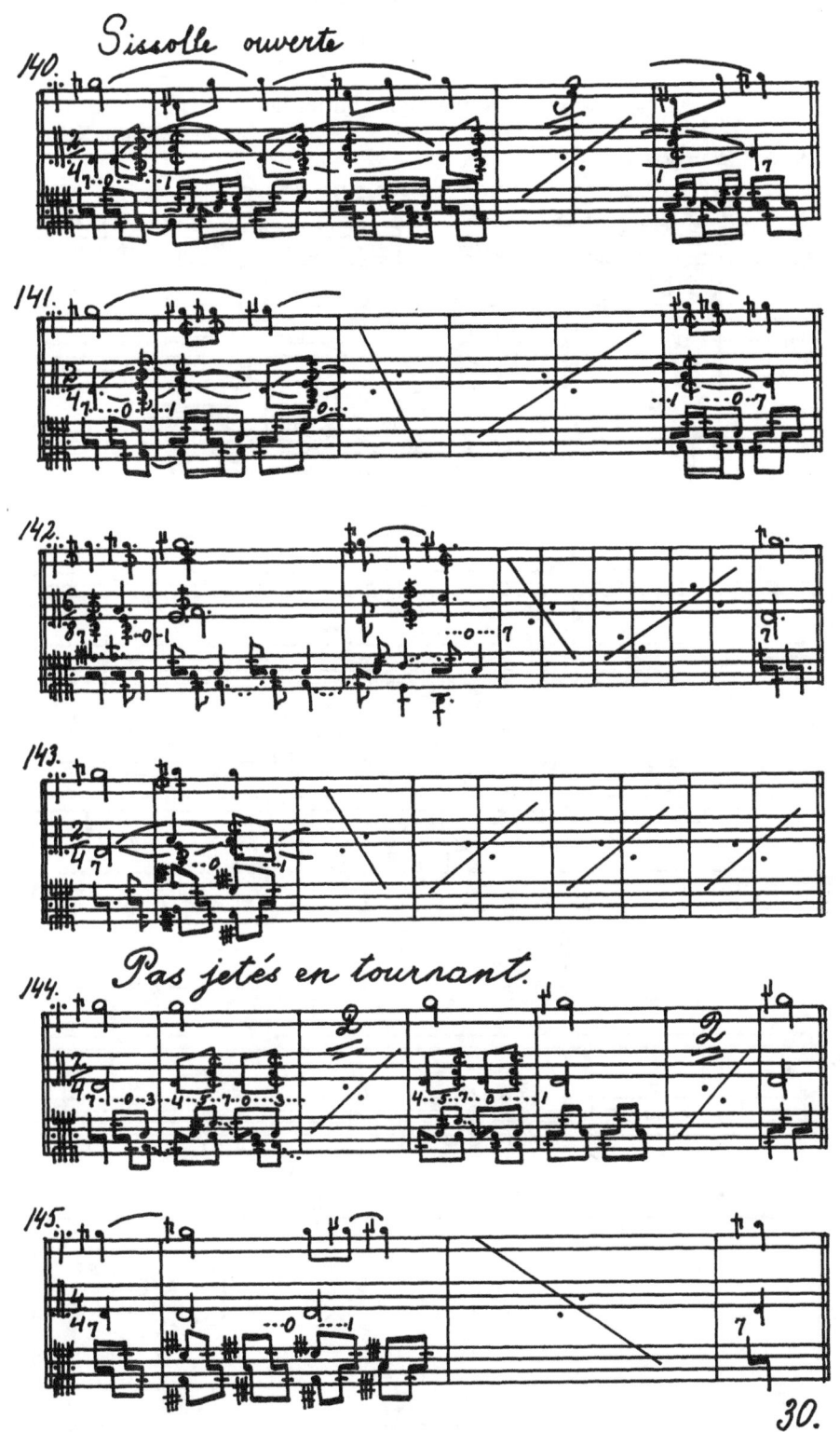

Excerpts from the ballet "Clorinda"
Composed by A. A. Gorsky

a. Awakening of the Alpine butterflies.

Music of Ernest Keller.

b. The appearance of Clorinda and the downfall of Franz, who is bewitched by her.

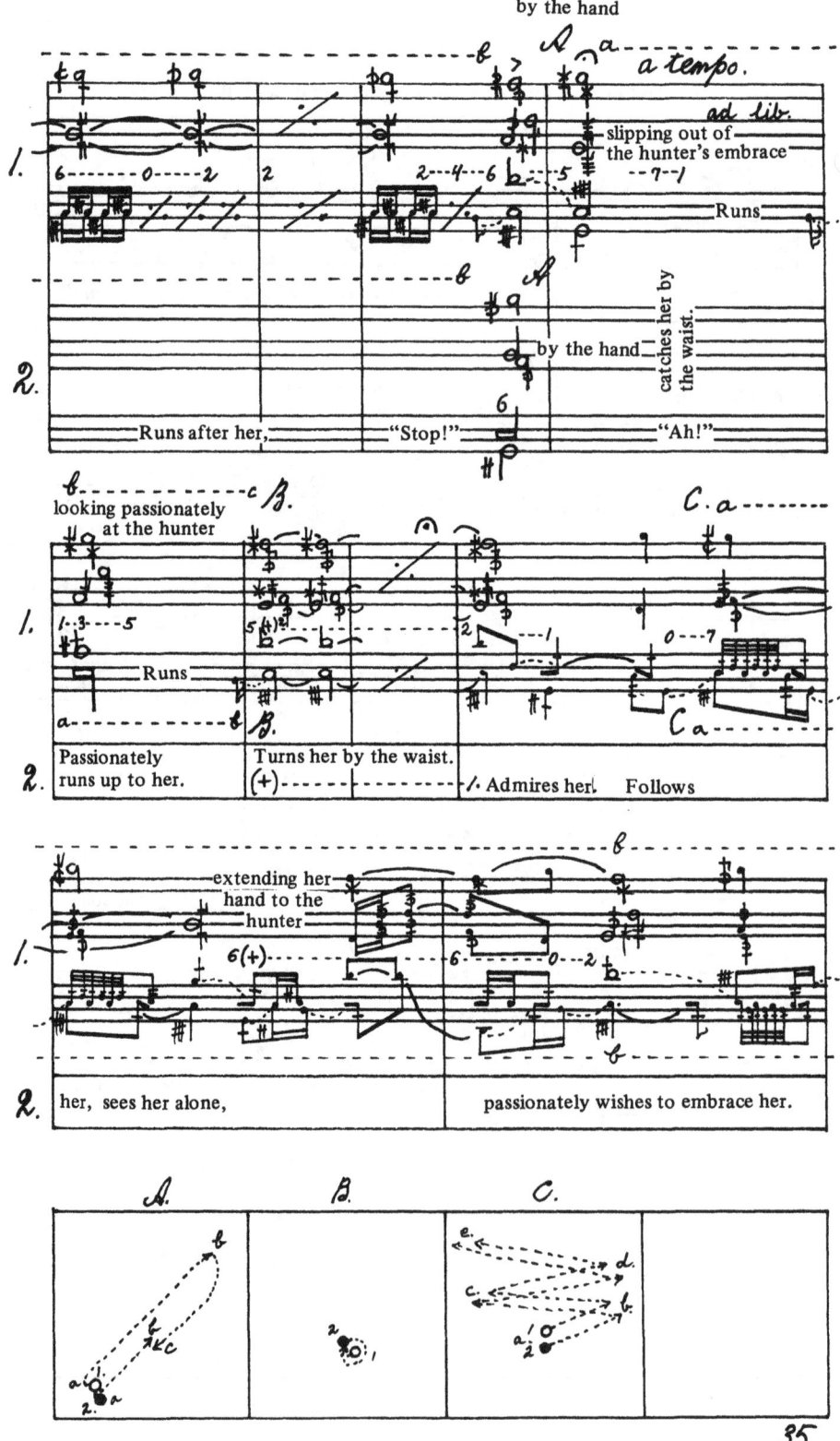

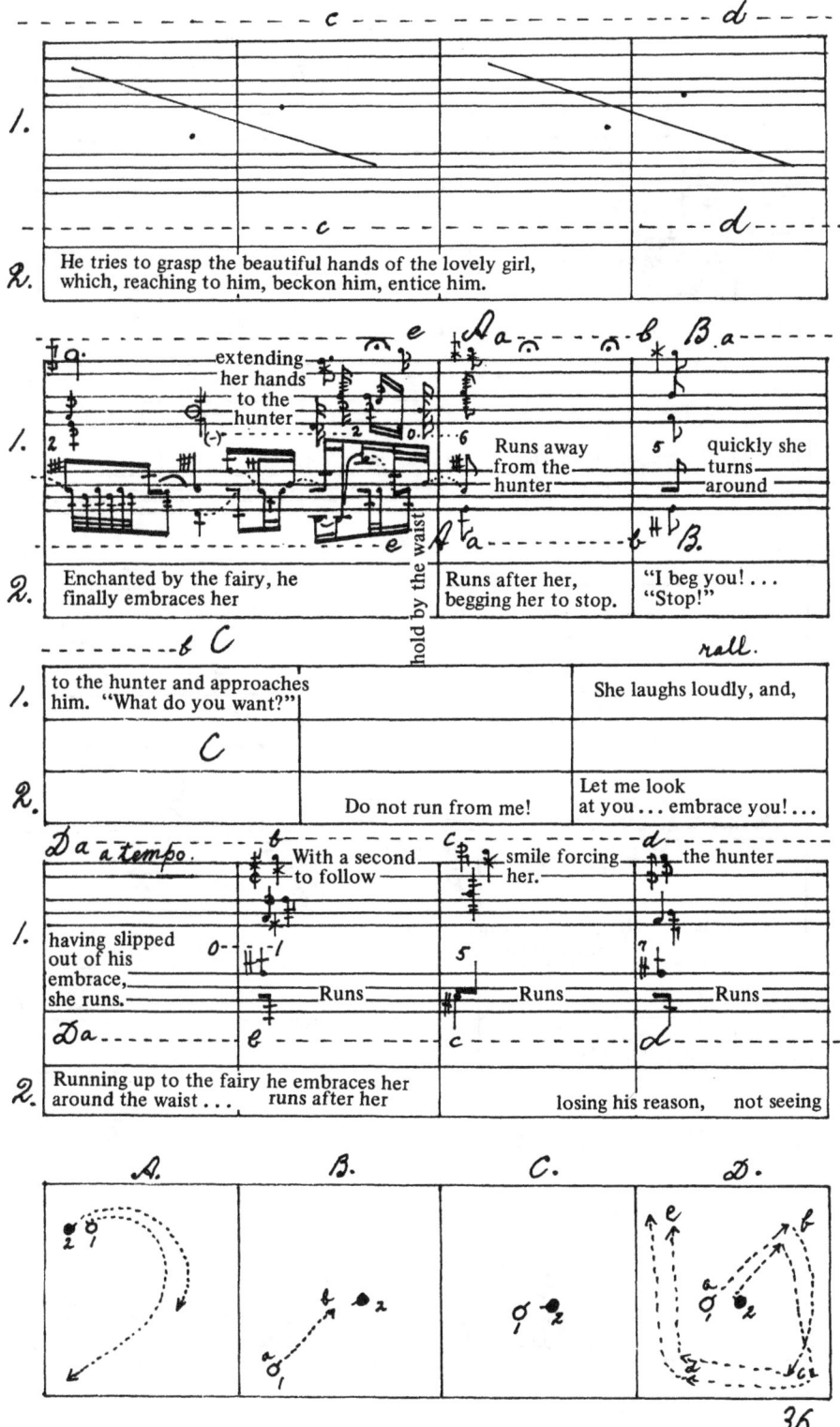

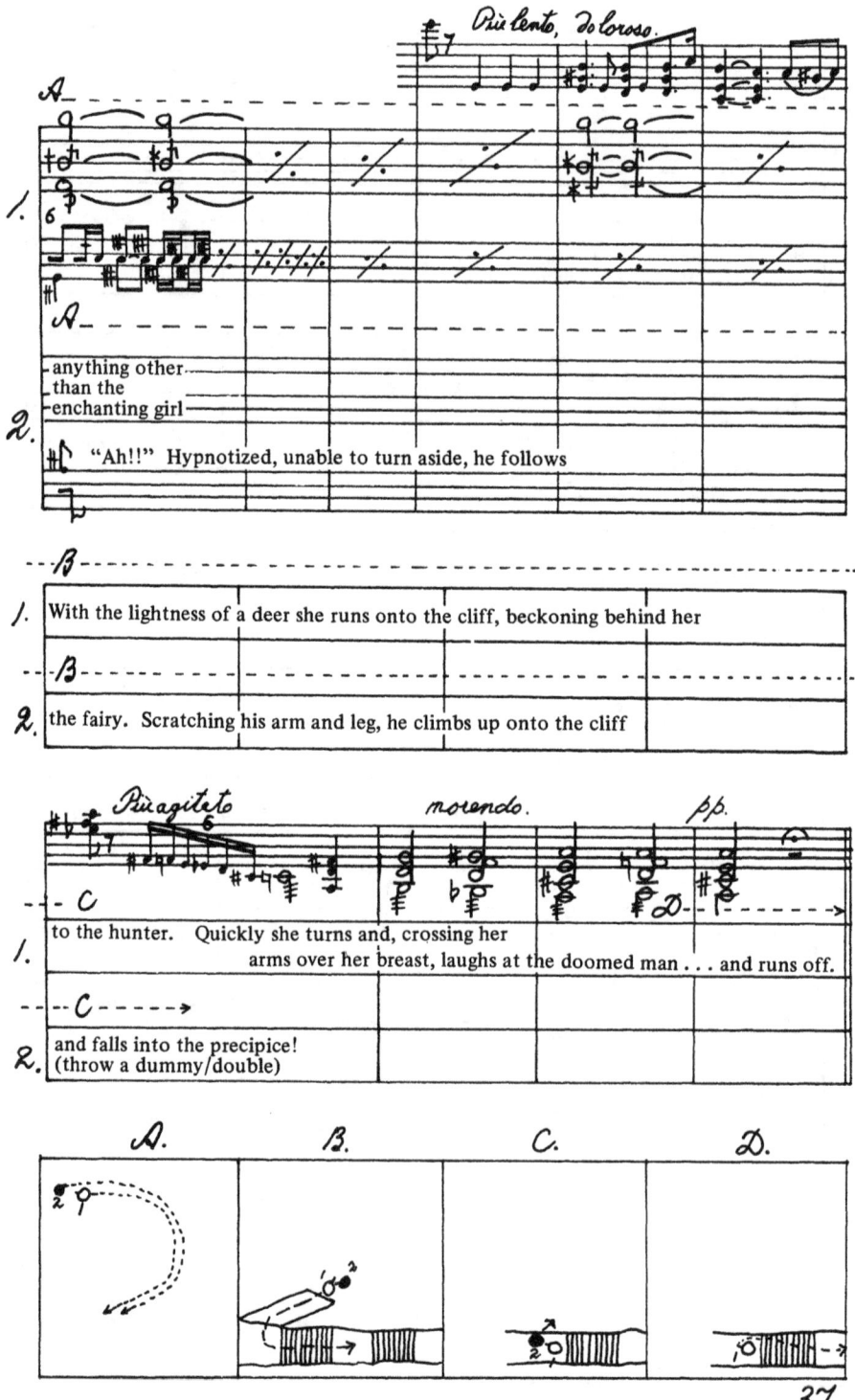

Man's variation

Comp. A. Gorsky
from Act III of the ballet:
"Swan Lake."

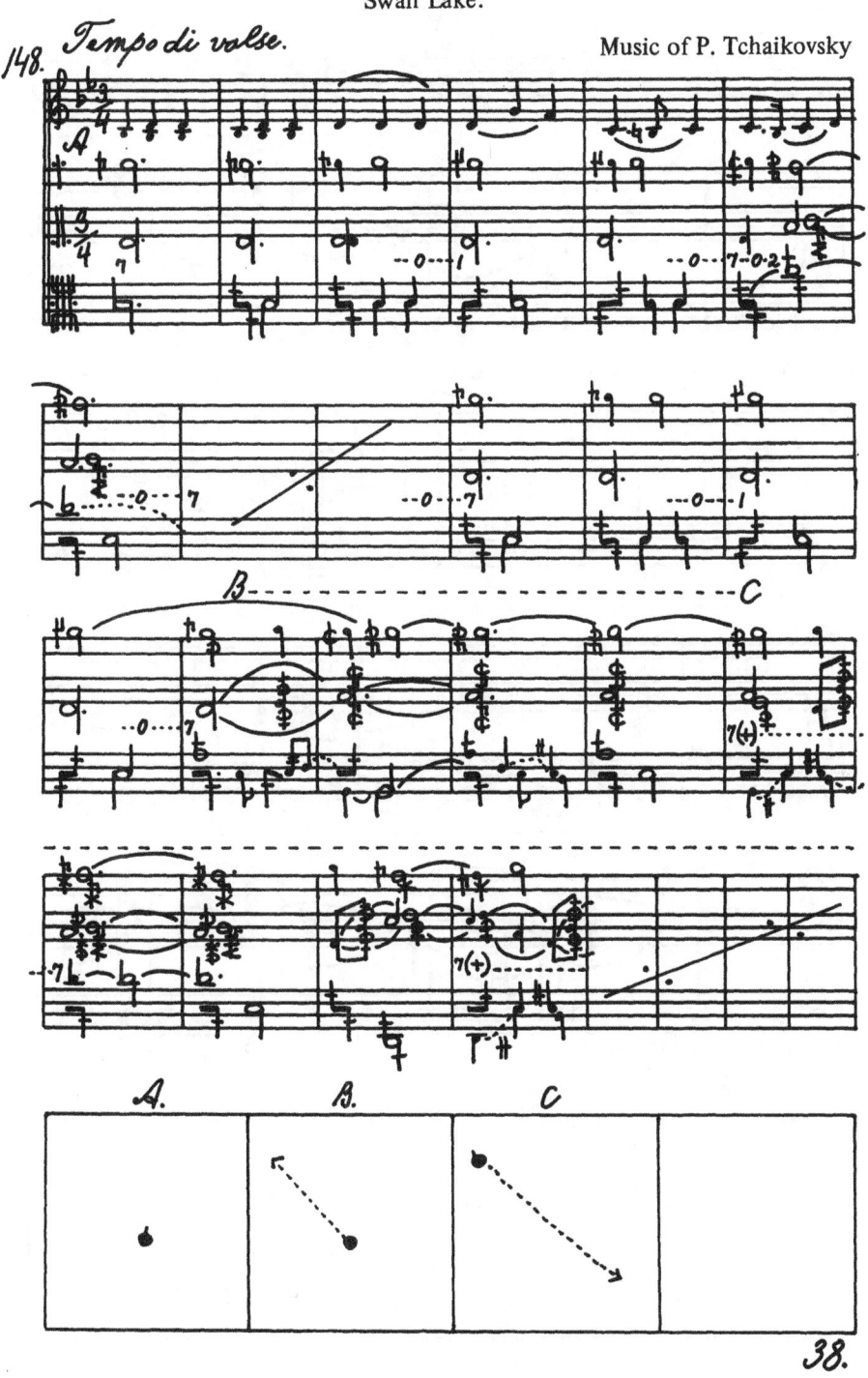

Music of P. Tchaikovsky

39.

Variation "Aurora"
Comp. M. Petipa
from Act I of the ballet:
"Sleeping Beauty."

Music of P. Tchaikovsky

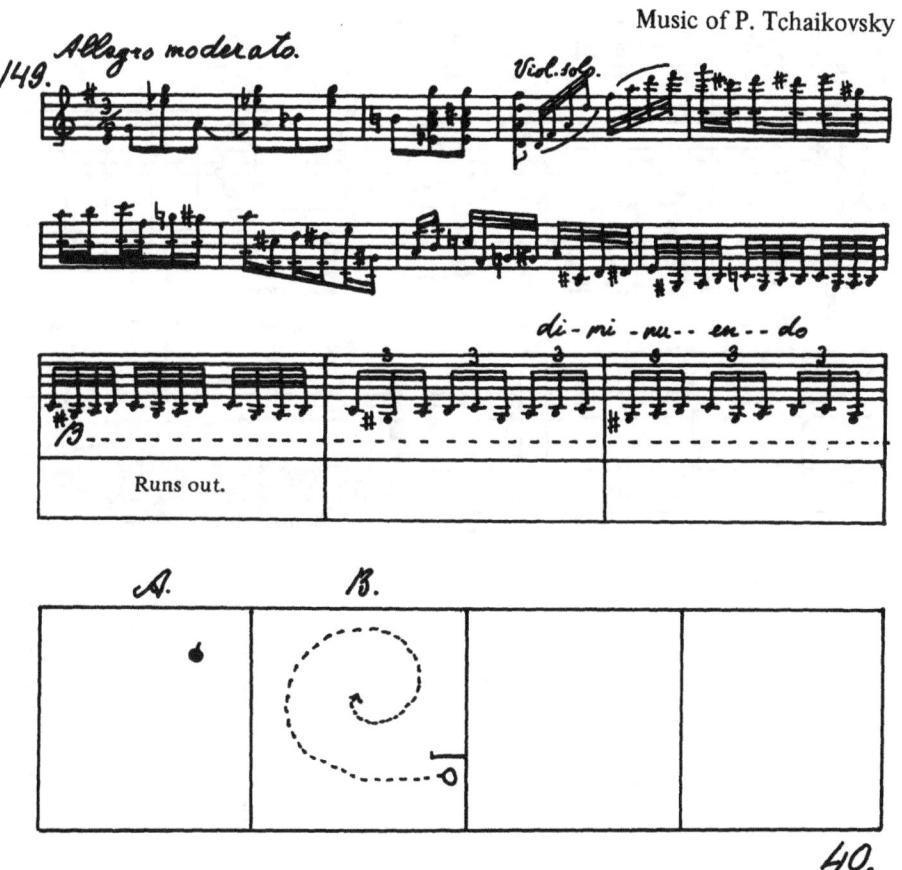

Runs out.

40.

[65]

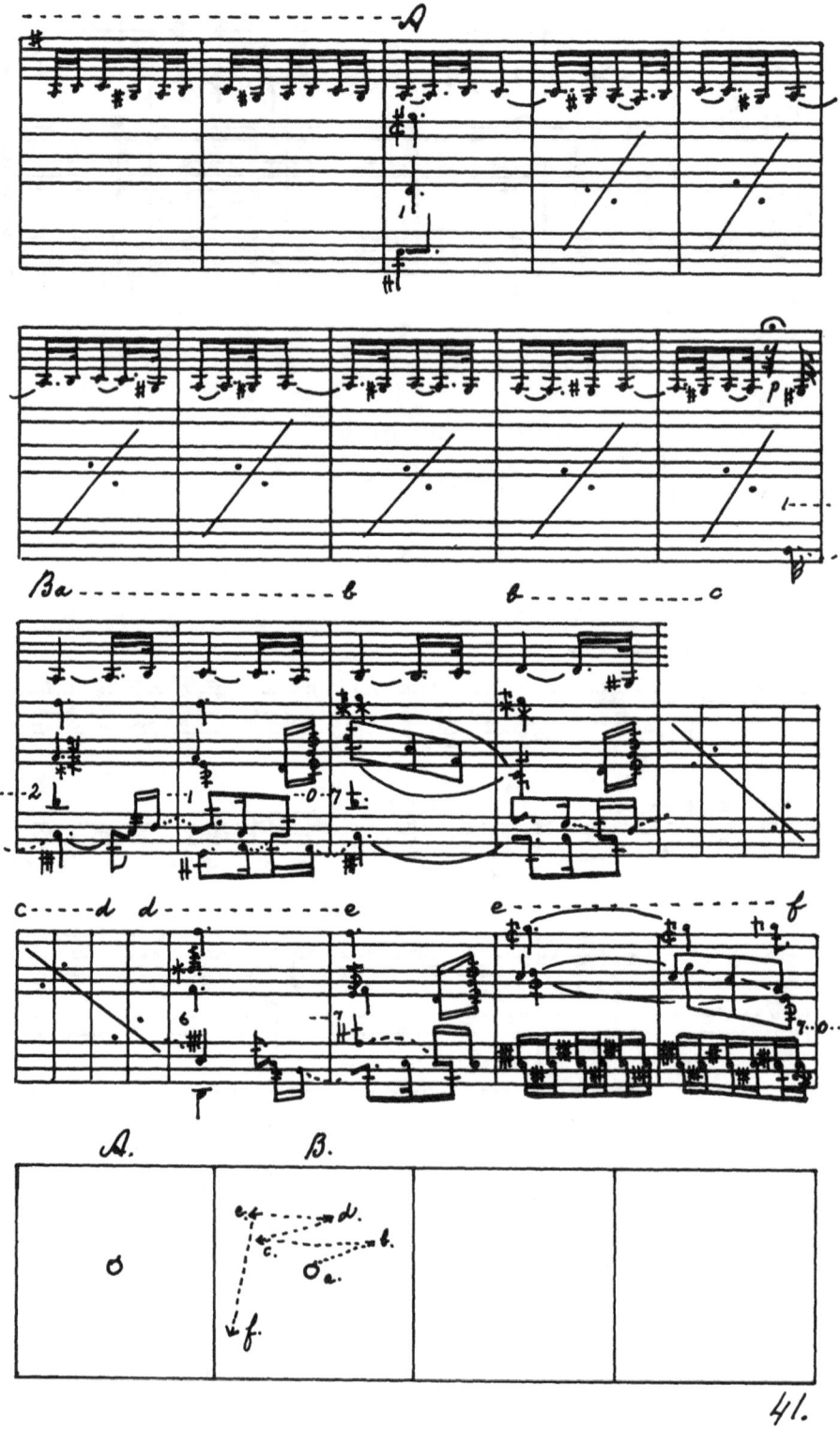

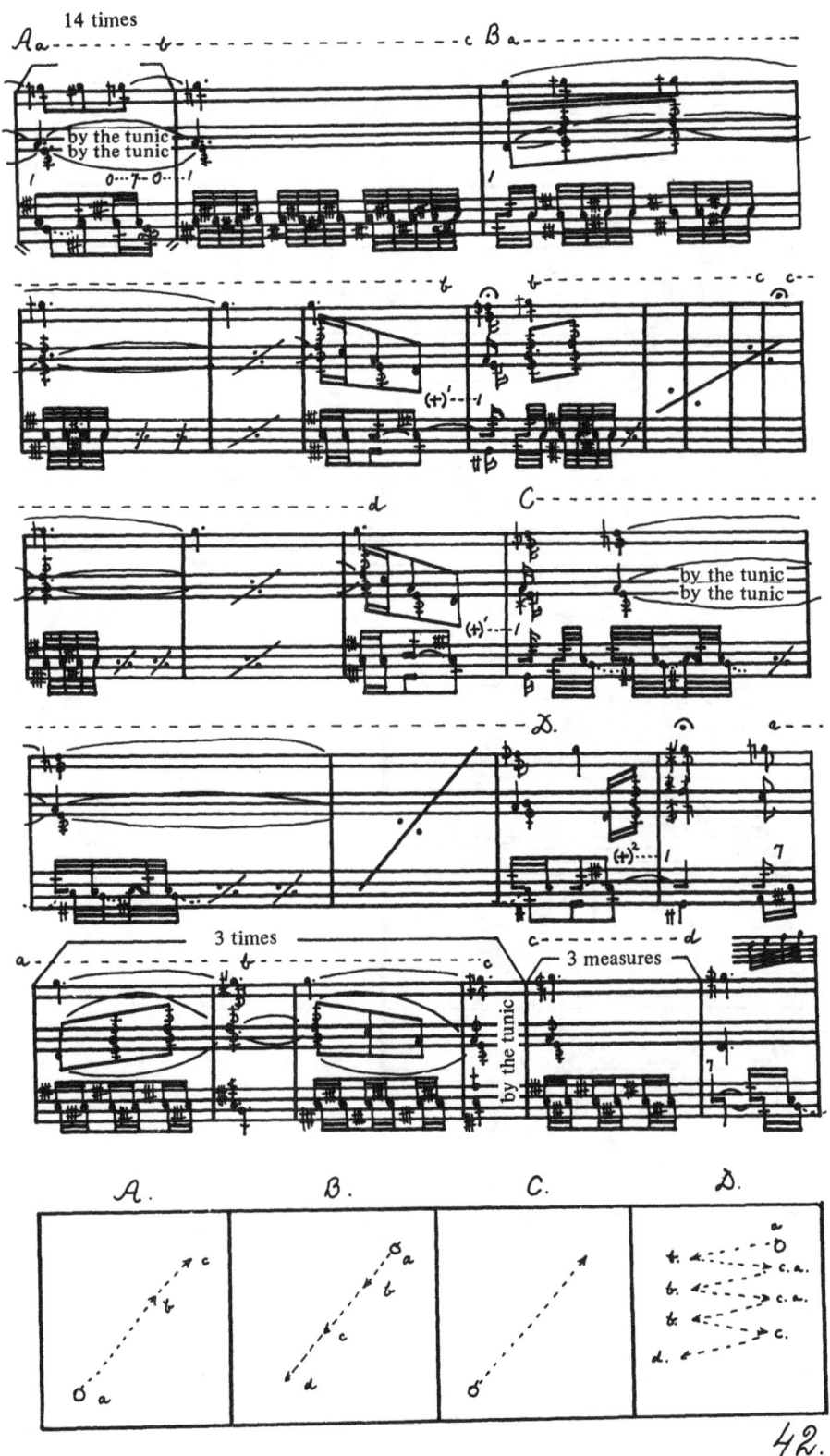

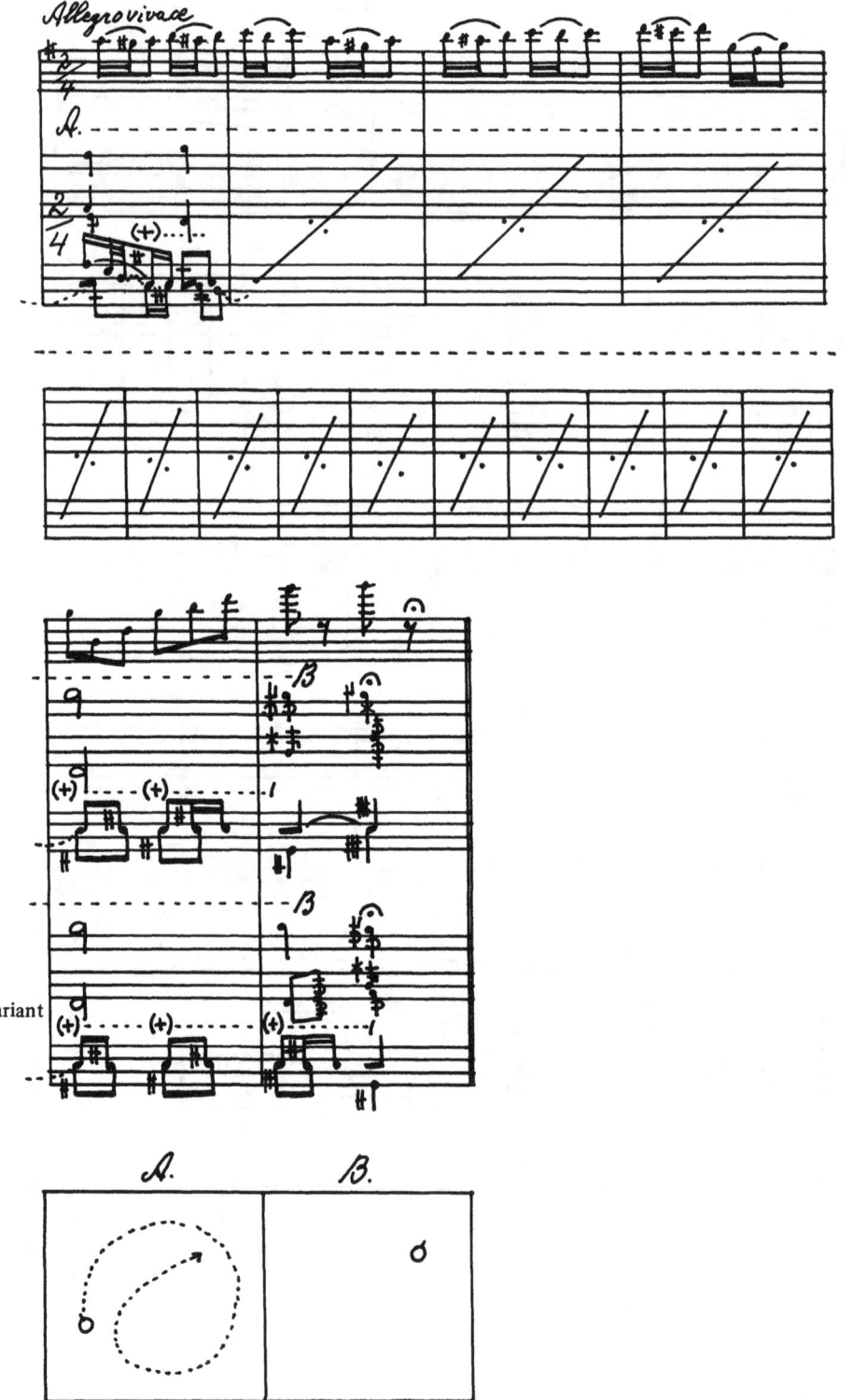

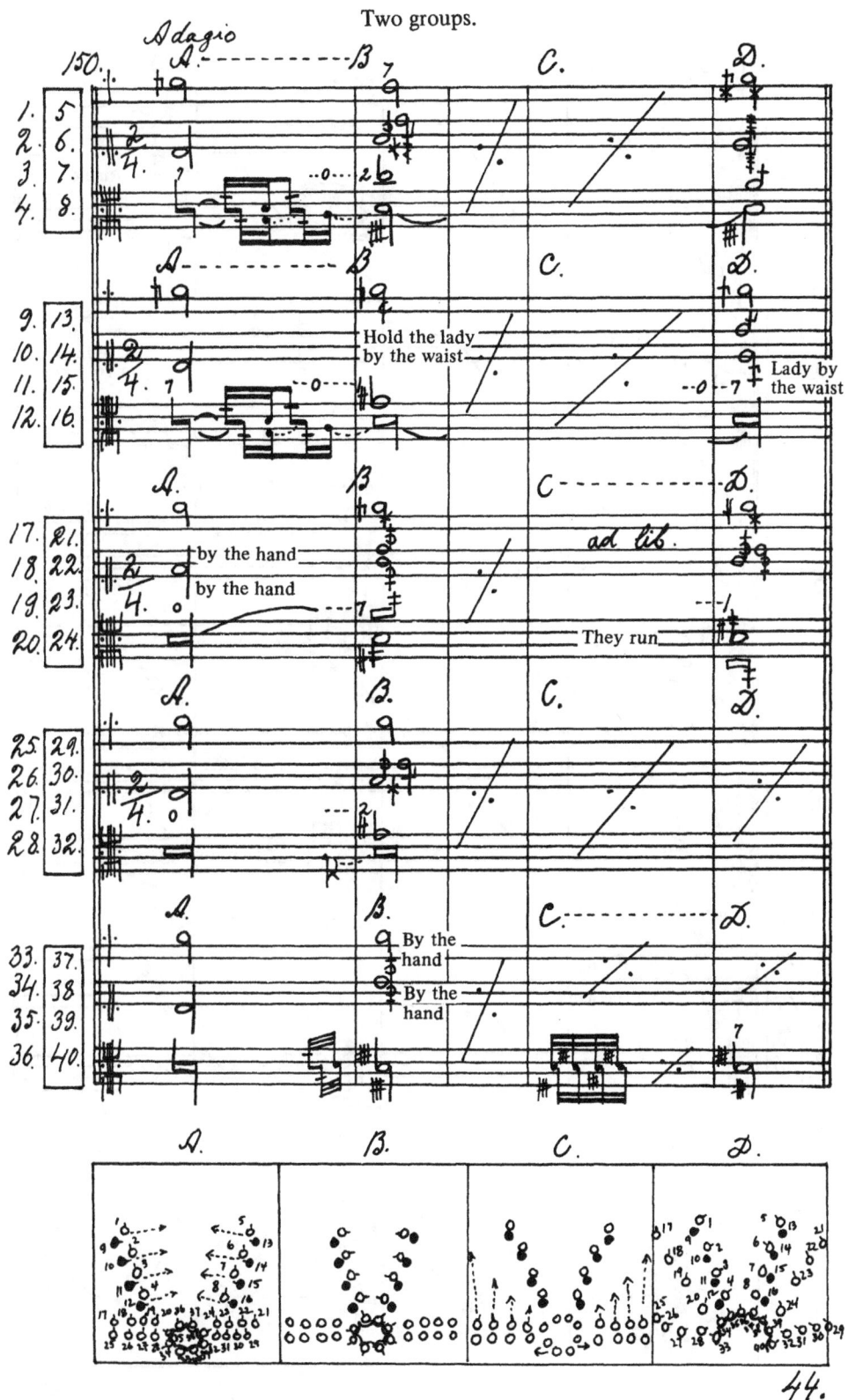

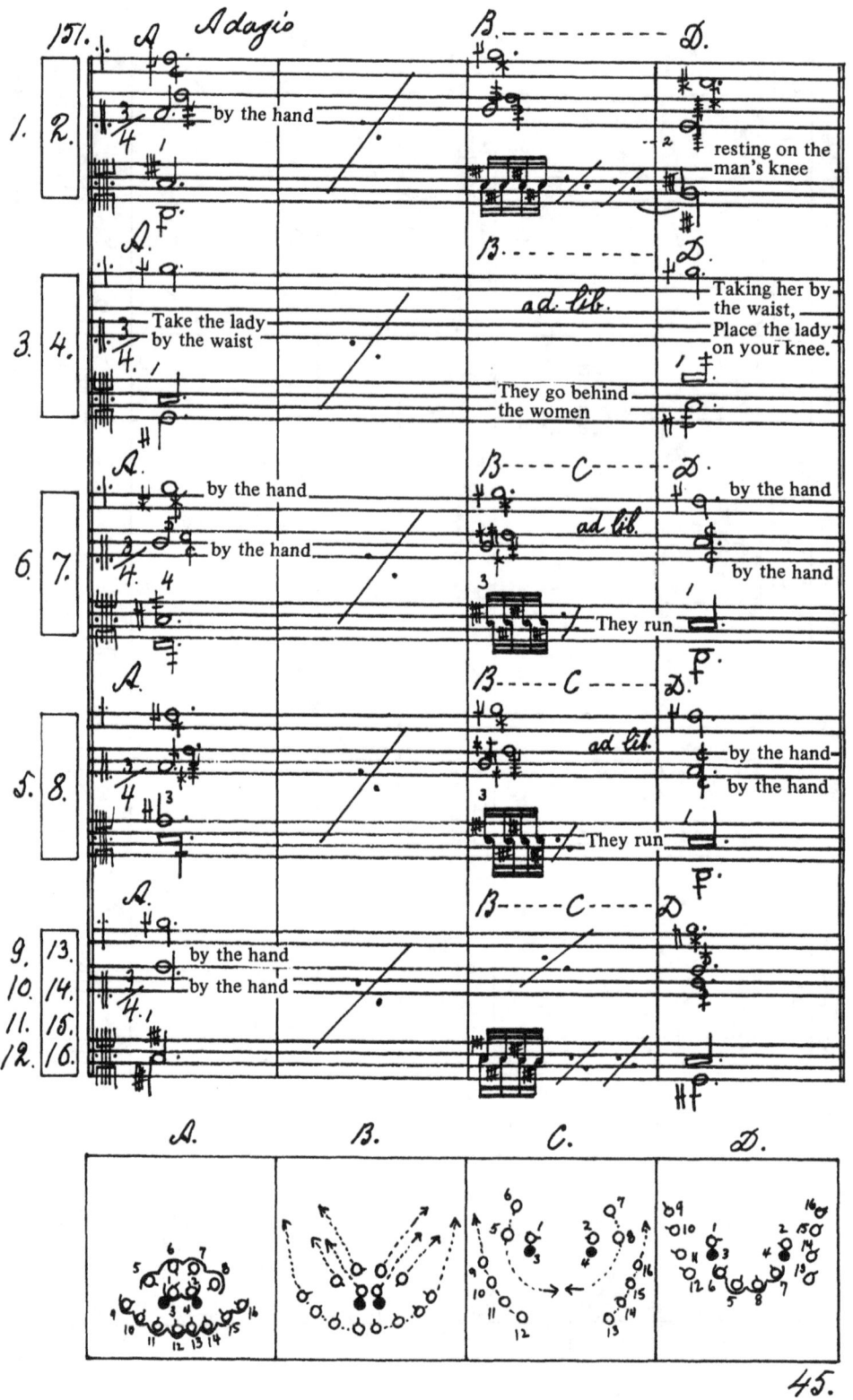

NOTES TO THE MAIN TEXT

¹ Gorsky's discussion of Arbeau is curious in that neither his description of Arbeau's method nor the example he provides is accurate. In what may be a typographical error he states that Arbeau's method "consists of *superscribing* comments *over* a musical note" [italics added], which has been corrected in this translation to conform with the example Gorsky provides. Moreover, the musical notation in Arbeau's treatise is typical of 16th-century prints, *i.e.*, it employs diamond-shaped note heads and not the square and round shapes that Gorsky uses. Finally, Arbeau's choreographies are not expressed in terms of *danse d'école*, as are Gorsky's. It would appear that Gorsky either misunderstood Arbeau or unwittingly used a corrupt edition.

² The printed text erroneously reads "six cervical vertebrae."

³ The reader will note that Gorsky has misplaced the label "10" in his drawings of the skeleton; this number should be at the front of the skeleton, not as he has it, pointing to the ischial tuberosities.

⁴ Gorsky has erred in this part of the description. The original reads: "Also connected to the torso are the shoulder blades (12), joined by appendages (12a), with the clavicles which, branching off from the upper part of the breastbone, and situated on the *back* and upper side of the torso, *along the sides of the spinal column,* serve as foundation for the upper extermities." Italics added.

⁵ In the original, the symbol on the left is in error, thus:

⁶ Reading down the page, the first eight examples illustrate symbols for the following:
    the whole leg en dehors at 45°
    the whole leg en dehors at 90°
    the whole leg en dedans at 45°
    the whole leg en dedans at 90°
    en dehors, knee at 90°
    en dedans, knee at 90°
    en dehors, knee at 135°
    en dedans, knee at 135°

⁷ In the original one symbol in the left column is in error:

⁸ In the original two symbols in the left column have the placement of flags reversed in error:

⁹ In the original two symbols in the left column have the placement of flags reversed in error:

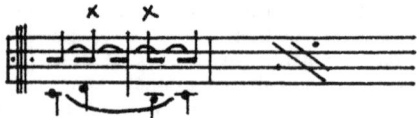

The reader will notice that Gorsky notated this example at 90° instead of 45°. In the original, moreover, this and the preceding entries in the "As Notated" column are reversed.

¹⁰ In the original the modifiers of the note symbol are in error:

¹¹ In the original the modifiers of the note symbol are in error:

¹² In the original one symbol is in error:

¹³ Reading down the page, the four examples of circular movements "in the shoulder joint" illustrate symbols for the following:
                en dehors at 45°
                en dedans at 45°
                en dehors at 90°
                en dedans at 90°

¹⁴ Reading down the page, the first four examples illustrate symbols for the following:
                arm to the side at 45°, the elbow en dehors at 135°
                arm to the side at 45°, the elbow en dedans at 135°
                arm to the side at 90°, the elbow en dehors at 135°
                arm to the side at 90°, the elbow en dedans at 135°

¹⁵ In the original the modifiers are in error:

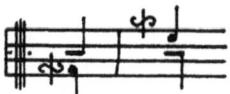

[16] In the original the modifier on the right is in error:

[17] In the original the modifiers are in error:

[18] In the original the modifiers are in error:

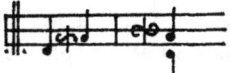

[19] This is not always true in practice. In the surviving manuscripts the dance notation may retain the quarter as a basic time unit in places where the music notation (supplied from an outside source) proceeds in larger or smaller basic pulses. See also example 146 of *Choreography*, in which Gorsky sets music in 2/4 to dance notation in 4/4.

AN ANNOTATED BIBLIOGRAPHY

Bakhrushin, Yurii Alekseevich. **Aleksandr Alekseevich Gorskii, 1871-1924.** Moscow and Leningrad: "Iskusstvo," 1946.

    A short biography (51 pp.), which includes an account of Gorsky's relationship to Stepanov and the notation system (pp. 10-14).

Borisoglebskii, M., compiler. **The Past of the Ballet Division of the Petersburg Theater School, now the Leningrad State Choreographic School. Materials for the History of Russian Ballet [Proshloe baletnogo otdeleniya peterburgskogo teatral'nogo uchilishcha, nyne Leningradskogo Gosudarstvennogo Khoregraficheskogo Uchilischcha. Materialy po istorii russkogo baleta].** 2 vols. Leningrad: Leningrad State Choreographic School, 1938-1939.

    An encyclopedic study of the St. Petersburg/Leningrad Ballet School, issued in celebration of its bicentennial. It contains biographical information all about graduates of the school for whom records survive, and is especially rich in data about salaries and promotions. Of interest to the present inquiry are:
        Vol. I, p. 308–biography of Stepanov.
        Vol. II, pp. 37-38–reminiscences of dancer Leonid Sergeyevich Leont'ev about Stepanov's notation system.
        Vol. II, p. 59–biography of Gorsky.
        Vol. II, pp. 76-79–biography of Sergeyev.
        Vol. II, pp. 260-262–Stepanov's program of classroom exercises for ballet training (mostly in French).

"Choreographic Notation [Khoreograficheskaya zapis']." **Moscow Gazette [Moskovskie vedomosti]**, 26 January 1899, p. 4, cols. 5-6.

    An unsigned account of the Gorsky production of *Sleeping Beauty* from notations, together with a biographical sketch of Stepanov.

Krasovskaya, Vera Mikhailovna. **Russian Ballet Theater of the Second Half of the Nineteenth Century [Russkii baletnyi teatr vtoroi poloviny XIX veka].** Moscow and Leningrad: "Iskusstvo," 1963.

    The standard Soviet history. Stepanov and his system are discussed on pp. 446-448.

_____. **Russian Ballet Theater of the Beginning of the Twentieth Century [Russkii baletnyi teatr nachala XX veka].** 2 vols. Leningrad: "Iskusstvo," 1971-1972.

    The latest installment in Krasovskaya's history, a continuation of the study cited next above. In her discussion of Gorsky as choreographer (I, 111-114), the author questions his exclusive reliance on Stepanov notations to produce both *Clorinda* and the Moscow *Sleeping Beauty*.

Lopukhov, Fedor Vasil'evich. **Candid Remarks About Choreography [Khoreograficheskie otkrovennosti]**. Moscow: "Iskusstvo," 1972.

    Diverse essays by the late Soviet choreographer; of particular interest is "About the System of Notating Movements" (pp. 52-54), in which the author disparages the Stepanov system.

_____. **Sixty Years in Ballet [Shest'desyat let v balete]**. Moscow: "Iskusstvo," 1966.

    Memoirs of the distinguished choreographer, who learned the Stepanov system as a student (under Nikolai Sergeyev) and a colleague of Gorsky. He writes of Gorsky's *Clorinda* on p. 134.

Notices of Stepanov's activities.

1. **Moscow Gazette [Moskovskie vedomosti]**, 25 February 1892, p. 4, col. 2.

   Reprint of extracts from **The New Time** article of 21 February 1892 (see No. 3 below).

2. **The New Time [Novoe vremya]**, 10 March 1891, p. 4, col. 3.

   Announcement of the invention of Stepanov's system and the appointment of a special commission to examine it.

3. **The New Time**, 21 February 1892, p. 4, col. 2.

   Announcement of the publication of Stepanov's book.

4. **The New Time**, 20 May 1892, p. 3, col. 5.

   Another announcement of the book; the system is to be taken up by "the famous balletmaster Rossi."

5. **The New Time**, 23 April 1893, p. 3, col. 5.

   Report of the second trial examination.

6. **The News and Mercantile Gazette [Novosti i birzhevaya gazeta]**, 19 September 1895, p. 3, cols. 2-3.

   Announcement of Stepanov's trip to Moscow to introduce the system in the Bolshoi Theater School.

Notices of Stepanov's death.

1. **The New Time**, 21 January 1896, p. 4, cols. 7-8.

2. **Theatergoer [Teatral]**, No. 54 (January 1896), p. 106.

3. **Yearbook of the Imperial Theaters [Ezhegodnik Imperatorskikh Teatrov]**, VI (Season 1895-1896), pp. 504-505.

Pchel'nikov, Pavel Mikhailovich. "Fate of a Talented Invention [Sud'ba odnogo talantlivogo izobreteniya]."

> A manuscript of eleven pages, as yet unpublished, about Stepanov and his notation system. "In connection with the fate of Stepanov and his invention the author touches on its uses, the condition of the imperial theaters' ballet and the theater school, speaks of the low level of culture of the workers of the ballet, and the mediocre level of education in the theater school."
> The manuscript is preserved at the State Central Theater Museum named for A. A. Bakhrushin, in Moscow; the description was cited from *Works of the State Central Theater Museum named for A. A. Bakhrushin* [Trudy Gosudarstvennogo Tsentral'nogo Teatral'nogo Muzeya im. A. A. Bakhrushina], ed. E. M. Kosolova and Vl. Filippov (Moscow and Leningrad: "Iskusstvo," 1941), pp. 208-209.

Roslavleva, Natalia Petrovna. **Era of the Russian Ballet.** New York: E. P. Dutton & Co., Inc., 1966.

> The standard English-language history of Russian ballet. Gorsky and Stepanov are discussed on pp. 156-158, Sergeyev's final days in Russia on pp. 197-198.

Slonimskii, Yurii Iosifovich, *et al.*, eds. **Marius Petipa. Materials, Recollections, Articles [Marius Petipa. Materialy, vospominaniya, stat'i].** Leningrad: "Iskusstvo," 1971.

> An excellent study of the famous balletmaster, which includes his diaries, autobiography, instructions to Tchaikovsky and Glazunov, sketches for a number of ballets, a bibliography, and his letter criticizing the Stepanov method (pp. 121-122). In one of the essays, Natalia Roslavleva establishes Petipa's birthdate.

Stepanov, V. I. **Alphabet of Movements of the Human Body. A study in recording the movements of the human body by means of musical signs.** Translated by Raymond Lister. Cambridge: The Golden Head Press, 1958; reprinted Brooklyn: Dance Horizons, 1969.

Stépanow, W. J. [= Stepanov, V. I.]. **Alphabet des mouvements du corps humain. Essai d'enregistrement des mouvements du corps humain au moyen des signes musicaux.** Paris: M. Zouckermann, 1892.

> The manual Stepanov published before returning to St. Petersburg. Published with it are a laudatory letter of Joseph Hansen and, in French, the first commission's certification of approval of the system.

Wiley, Roland John. "Dances From Russia: An Introduction to the Sergejev Collection." **Harvard Library Bulletin,** XXIV (1976), 94-112.

> A short biography of Nikolai Sergeyev and a description of his collection of documents pertaining to Russian ballet.

www.ingramcontent.com/pod-product-compliance
Lightning Source LLC
Chambersburg PA
CBHW082104280426
43661CB00089B/855